A Door of Hope

Robert Thornton Henderson

A Door of Hope

Spiritual Conflict in Pastoral Ministry

Wipf and Stock Publishers
150 West Broadway • Eugene OR 97401
2001

A Door of Hope
Spiritual Conflict in Pastoral Ministry
By Henderson, Robert

ISBN: 1-57910-737-0

Reprinted by *Wipf and Stock Publishers*
150 West Broadway • Eugene OR 97401

Previously published by Herald Press, 1997.

To Grover and Helena, Nat and Mary,
whose faithfulness
as kingdom pastors in difficult places
gives heart to so many of us.
They are instruments of God's praise,
for whom I am profoundly thankful.

Contents

Preface

WRITING and teaching, especially on a topic such as spiritual conflict in pastoral ministry, dare not be done in a vacuum. Amid the daily stresses and opportunities of pastoral ministry, the writer-teacher needs meetings with God on emotionally real islands of Patmos (see Rev. 1).

I'm not impressed by those who avoid intractable pastorates or whose charismatic personalities excite congregations briefly as they move up. I am thankful for them and their gifts, but I don't identify with them. I hope that doesn't sound like sour grapes. Bookstores are full of success stories. They only leave the rest of us more frustrated.

Thousands of dreary congregations don't remember or expect anything else. A new pastor comes along periodically, like a new coat of paint on the sanctuary wall. There is brief respite from sameness, but gray soon returns.

Everything I write here is out of my own agony, excitement, adventure, and lifelong study of the mystery and disciplines of congregational renewal. My thinking emerges especially from my own tradition and its many nearly dead congregations. The situation is not unique to mainline churches. I have seen it in other denominations and settings; it is experienced by all who want to pastor with integrity.

After beginning my ordained career in the glamour of campus ministry, I was called (abandoned?) by God to a no-person's-land congregation in a small southern city. That was my moment of truth. Could I even trust God there? Could I find guidance and principle in Scripture to help me know what God's purpose was for such an apparently God-forsaken place?

Today I place high value on those nine years. Two things were God's provision for me. At a formative Bible conference, I had been taught and mentored concerning the spiritual conflict which involves all Christians. Without that preparation, I doubt that I would have survived. I also was ten minutes from a major divinity school and its library, where I could probe and study the subject.

In addition, God shut me up in a place where I could only engage in the spiritual formations of desperate prayer, dwelling in the secret place, waiting for some divine solution to my dilemma. I found riches under strange rocks! What emerged was a *pattern given on the mount.* This pattern is not dramatic or new, but it served me in a struggling congregation in that southern textile village as well as in a deteriorating neighborhood at the heart of a major city. More recently the pattern served me in a large congregation at a lovely mountain resort and retirement community. That congregation had endured a traumatic and destructive crisis several months before I was asked to come. Unresolved conflicts and pathologies awaited me.

From 1975 to 1978, I was staff person in evangelism for the Presbyterian Church, U.S. (Southern). Though I was serving a denomination not renowned for its evangelistic creativity or fruitfulness, I traveled to scores of congregations and presbyteries to listen, discuss, teach, and equip. I participated in ecumenical councils and evangelical associations dealing with evangelism and church renewal. I lectured on evangelism and defended it in seminaries not always congenial to the subject.

I learned that healthy congregations produce spontaneous and healthy evangelistic outreach. It is a dirty trick to try to hang a program of evangelistic outreach on a sick congregation and lure unsuspecting outsiders into pathological congregations, hoping they may remedy the illnesses! However, churches that are wholesome and fruitful in evangelistic outreach do experience tensions and subtle conflicts. In recent years I have focused on the possibility that pastors can be midwives of renewal in sick congregations.

One often hears evangelical churches contrasted with mainline churches. This is simplistic. I am Presbyterian—about as mainline as one can get. Yet for all this denomination's public image, it includes every shade of biblical interpretation. Like most mainline denominations, it has a traditional and confessional position in form and constitution, but it is many generations from its roots. On one hand, the denomination includes fundamentalists; on the other hand, some have forsaken biblical canonicity and creedal affirmations. In between are many positions. Congregations find resources to suit their own doctrinal and ideological personalities.

In my career I have been in contact with a range of church traditions. In all of them I find the spiritual warfare this book addresses. Because of my interest, study, and experience, I am in conversation with many pastors from several denominational traditions who feed me data as well as heartbreak. Therefore, I do not write in a vacuum.

I also write with passion to bring instruction and encouragement to faithful and despairing brothers and sisters in difficult pastoral assignments. Most of all, when God's name is on a church, God's honor and glory are at stake. I have to believe God has a purpose for all the sterile ecclesiastical scenes, all the congregations experiencing evangelical amnesia. God wants them to come alive again and to become demonstrations of new creation.

This is not an easy book. North American churches have been lulled into a stupor with regard to the spiritual context of our culture. Spiritual realities take on different appearances in different cultures and settings. As North America wrestles with secularism and as cultural violence becomes more apparent, it may be increasingly difficult and even perilous to be a pastor with *kingdom integrity.* The ideologies of the dominant social order are vigorous and well rooted. More and more they possess the church. What energizes these aims of self-fulfillment, greed, market capitalism, its companions of consumerism and materialism, its nationalism, and its ethnic and gender isms? What is the spiritual reality of these expressions?

I resonate with Dr. Neuza Itioka, Brazilian missionary.

> Certainly one of the most important issues worldwide missions must face in the 1990s is how to confront the destructive supernatural evil forces that oppose the missionary enterprise. For too long the Western church has tended toward an intellectual expression of its faith, failing to confront realistically the supernatural manifestations.[1]

I also recognize that Satan, the god of this age, seeks to blind every mind (2 Cor. 4:4). The evil one is grasping to control the whole cosmos. Amid church conflicts, we are dealing not just with human gifts and skills or their lack, but with a counterfeit religion lacking biblical integrity. The real renewal of the church into kingdom wholeness, whether Catholic or Protestant, liberal or conservative, Pentecostal or evangelical, will come with some basic conflict between gospel and culture (Matt. 10:34).

The conflict is fed by a battle behind the battle. Behind the normal application of human skills in creating wholesome congregations, there lurks a clandestine and energized evil which aims to subvert those efforts and render them fruitless. We must address this evil. I want to call the church to a new understanding of pastoral ministry, a new pastoral definition. This will require looking at the church with different eyes. This is also a wake-up call!

I thank God for saints who have discipled and mentored me over these decades, especially the godly folk of the Peniel Bible Conference. I thank God for many prayer partners whose intercessions have sustained me. I also thank my wife and co-worker, Betty. She has prayed with me and for me. She has lived with me and encouraged me through times of spiritual depression and dark nights of the soul. Finally, I thank my colleague Chuck Guth, who kept me company through nightmarish conflict times—and helped me with word processing this book.

—Robert T. Henderson
Ramah on Harbour Oaks Road
Tucker, Georgia

1

Kingdom and Conflict in Pastoral Ministry

ANNIE DILLARD tells of walking by her Tinker Creek one summer day and noticing something appalling. A green frog, half out of water, deflated before her eyes until nothing was left but green skin floating like scum on the water. She had observed the work of a giant waterbug. The waterbug, she explains, is a huge, heavy-bodied brown beetle which eats insects, tadpoles, fish, and frogs. It puts pincers into the victim, then inserts an enzyme which dissolves the insides. The giant waterbug sucks out the results and has a hearty meal![1]

I ponder this episode as I watch with increasing sadness the great host of dispirited pastors in the Christian church. For every pastor who professes to be fulfilled and joyous in pastoral ministry, there are a score who with the psalmist lament,

> I am in pain and distress. (Ps. 69:29)
> Hasten, O God, to save me;
> O Lord, come quickly to help me. (Ps. 70:1)

> All my enemies are before you.
> Scorn has broken my heart
> and has left me helpless;
> I looked for sympathy, but there was none,
> for comforters, but I found none. (Ps. 69:19-20)

Mirth, joy, gladness, thanksgiving, praise, timbrel, and dance are irresistibly sucked out of them. With glazed eyes they go through the motions of clergy maintenance work. They become empty forms floating on the stream.

There seldom appears to be a satisfying alternative. It is all so inexplicable. It seemed so good and right at the beginning—an act of faith and devotion, a divine call, the affirmation of Christian friends. Now something seems so wrong. If they turn back from pastoring, they raise doubts about themselves, God, and the church; they incur the misunderstanding and shaking heads of family and friends.

What has happened? What giant waterbug has dissolved one's insides and filled one with frustration, doubt, despair, hopelessness? Does God abandon congregations? Does God abandon pastors? Has God abandoned me?

Three friends who graduated from theological school ten years ago came from wholesome Christian backgrounds. They entered seminary out of real conviction and an inner sense of calling, out of a desire to praise their Lord Jesus Christ through pastoral ministry, affirmed by their Christian communities. Though they had not known each other previously, they became inseparable. They were in a large Bible study group and were faithful prayer partners for each other. All three were tennis buffs who would pick up anyone available for a set of doubles. Their hearts were bonded.

Ben, Debbie, and Andy had different temperaments, but their lives intertwined. Late evenings after time in the library, they would go out for pizza and dream of what lay before them. They shared discoveries and regaled each other with new insights into *Heilgeschichte*[2] and the kingdom of God. They talked excitedly about curricular projects.

Ben was a jock, a natural leader, good-looking, charming, at ease among people anywhere, and enthusiastic. He had studied business administration in college. After a short career with a major corporation, he pursued pastoral ministry. Debbie was attractive, intense, and disciplined. She had been a sorority leader at the university and had a degree in education. She had natural communication gifts, winning ways, and a wholesome appreciation for the place of women in ministry. Andy was cerebral. Although athletic, he was shy, reflective, insightful, and analytical. He had twin majors in philosophy and history. He had taught high school for two years before seminary.

In their final seminary year, they prayed together about where they might be going and which churches would call them. They shared their anxieties, joked together, and had a sense of expectancy. Ben was called to be associate pastor in a "tall steeple" (large and prosperous) church in a distant city. He married his high school sweetheart and was immediately swept into the heart of the congregation. His managerial gifts were obvious in his ability to organize and expedite congregational ministries. His popularity was known churchwide. It was no surprise that after four years he became senior pastor of another "tall steeple" church, where his popularity was undiminished. Ben became a favorite on the conference circuit. He was a "success."

Debbie was called to a 250-member congregation in a small suburban town. As their first woman pastor, she was wonderfully received and appreciated. Her gifts emerged naturally. She sought with integrity to implement ministries of worship, using all of her skills in liturgics but even more to enliven the congregation's educational ministries. She was diligent. However, the congregation resisted the reality of the faith. The members were accustomed to young and imaginative clergy coming to them and trying out their ideas, so they let Debbie work. Yet they never seemed to see beyond the surface of proposed changes.

Andy took a small church in an industrial community. He believed these non-prestigious congregations were worthy of good ministry. He had no aspirations to be an ecclesiastical climber. He relished the challenge of a congregation of folk who also were not social climbers but were hardworking and genuine. He was convinced that good teaching would effect a quickening in the congregation. The smallness of the congregation would provide him the time to read and reflect that a larger and more demanding congregation would not. After several years, Andy entered a doctor of ministry program and sharpened his church administration skills.

Ten years passed, during which these old friends were only occasionally in touch. Then they all attended a church conference at a denominational retreat center. In the registration line, they stumbled across each other. Over supper that first night, the years faded as they shared pilgrimages.

Ben confessed that he had been swept along by the affirmation and popularity he enjoyed. When he slowed down long enough to reflect on who he was and where he was going, he would ask himself, *What has all of this to do with my vision?* The vision of the community of the kingdom of God seemed to recede further and further. He felt seduced but unable to change course.

In Andy's pilgrimage, the more he read, the more he became excited about the gospel and the church. Some members sensed his excitement and in response began to see with new eyes. Outwardly, the church was doing well, and people appreciated his gentle pastoral skills. Still, Andy noted that at critical junctures key members would stonewall steps of congregational growth and obedience. Most of the congregation's images and understanding of the Christian message seemed to come from somewhere else. Idols not easily definable possessed the hearts of the congregation. That frustrated Andy's finely tuned spirit.

Debbie had been a workaholic. Without admitting it to herself until now, she had had to prove to herself that women in ministry are a significant part of church life. She nurtured all the structures she knew to be necessary in a living church, but hardly anyone seemed to care. They did admire her for her zeal and ability. They spoke well of her and invited friends to become part of the church. They participated dutifully if indifferently. She told Ben and Andy that she and the congregation were on different wavelengths. They had a warm and loving relationship but spoke different languages. Her only recourse was to keep up a holy resolve, yet she lacked expectation for true renewal.

There was a break in the afternoon schedule on the next day of the conference. The three friends agreed to pursue the conversation on a hike up a mountain trail. It was a spectacular time of the year, the rhododendrons were in bloom, and the joy of seeing each other and being able to talk freely and honestly made this time precious.

Here were *Seduction, Frustration,* and *Resolution* personified, walking together and looking again at the Vision.[3] The church, the pastoral ministry—what was it all about? It all looked so proper, so tame, so religious, so powerless, so much a part of "everything else" in society, so disconnected from God's Vision for the world. Each young pastor had been diligent. Each had labored unto weariness and had given it their best shot. Yet. . . .

Andy, typically, verbalized his sneaking suspicion

that pastoral ministry as he was practicing it was based on the wrong foundation. He had found a statement by an obscure theologian, Franz Overbeck, who was convinced that all church theology and self-understanding had gone off track after its first few centuries. From that time on, the church has been un-Christian, even satanic, drawing Christianity into the sphere of civilization, into the culture of the "age of death." In so doing, the church has denied the essentially prophetic and forward-looking character of the Christian faith and of the kingdom of God or "the age to come."[4]

"Could it be," Andy asked his companions, "that somehow we are looking at the church as mere humans, and missing altogether the relationship of the church to the reign of God in Jesus Christ?" Debbie and Ben listened but could only respond that they simply wished they again had their earlier excitement about Jesus and love for him.

They shared and talked and joked as they walked that mountain trail. At the top, they grew silent. Each looked off at distant ridges and peaks, pondering thoughts too deep for words. On a stone outcropping at the edge of a field of blueberries, they prayed together again as they had not prayed in ten years. When they finished, they were weeping.

The three returned to the conference and to their congregations, mostly in silence and with some sadness. Something in them died a little because they had seen the Vision slip a little further from their grasp. They had reminded each other of the Vision, but none of them sensed any real participation in it. A little more of their insides had been sucked out. It seemed so irreversible.

These three pastors are a composite of real persons with whom I continue to have vital relationships. In this book, I will use my ongoing friendship with them as a literary device. I trust my readers will indulge my effort to keep the document alive and fully engaged with reality.

I invite you to join my conversations with these friends. After the episode on the mountaintop, I joined the discussions. Sometimes these were at periodic retreats, which we cherished as times to encourage each other to maintain the integrity of our ministries in light of the Vision. Our dialogue is interspersed throughout this book.

There are risks to this approach. This book is intended to be a perilous and exciting attempt to open eyes to see the future that God wills. When the Vision is dynamic, real, and formative, pastoral ministry can become the arena that helps kingdom communities to emerge.

My three friends belong to the same mainline denomination, but their congregations represent three types. Ben's is the *large, prosperous* congregation that essentially does what it wants and pays nominal respect to the denomination. Though loyal to the denomination at one level, it carries on its own congregational enterprise almost independently. It networks with similar large urban congregations in other denominations.

Debbie's congregation is *loyal to the denomination and its program.* It responds to denominational agendas, its members serve on denominational committees, and it primarily looks to the denomination for its resources. Yet it sometimes questions the integrity and fruitfulness of the resources supplied.

Andy's is the *conservative evangelical* congregation. Though denominational, its resources come from evangelically oriented presses and parachurch agencies. It maintains its denominational ties but often feels like an alien minority in the denomination.

Pastor personalities vary. Ben is the extrovert. He has charisma and is by nature entrepreneurial. He pastors what might be called a *megachurch.* As such, he is a member of the Rotary and the country club, where he regularly plays golf with members. Debbie is sensitive to people, intuitive, and committed to integrity. Her congregation is more accustomed to saluting the denominational structures and programs than are Ben's or Andy's. This at times challenges her integrity. Andy is the reflective and poetic introvert. He confronts conservative forces at work in his congregation, whose members like to hear the evangelical code words and familiar church language of yesterday.[5]

While there is always conflict caused by human differences and variations in pastoral and administrative gifts, there is also more. There is the *battle behind the battle:* demonic irrationality, a subtle, malignant, and never-ending opposition to the development of fruitful and obedient congregations submitted to the dominion of God. Yes, something satanic is at work. The prince of darkness cleverly filters out the radical otherness, the eschatological[6] nature of the kingdom of God. This leaves the church and pastoral ministry with the form of Christian faith but not its power, making the church an expression of *this evil age* rather than serving *the age to come,* which is God's reign.

Second, I want to redefine pastoral ministry in terms of deliberate martyrdom, of conflict in a redemptive warfare, of the thrilling adventure of walking the boundary between the *age of death* and the *age to come,* and of calling and re-calling the church to its *kingdom consciousness.*

Who is my audience? I want to reach disillusioned, lonely pastors from myriad congregations and denominations, who weep and wonder how to sing the Lord's song in an alien land. I want to reach the godly, well-intentioned, but ineffective ones who pray and yearn for something better, yet live in unreality, going through motions, preaching sermons, performing the expected custodial duties, never seeing the Vision of the pattern given on the mount.

Finally, I want to reach the godly laity who hurt for their pastors and wonder how to encourage and support them. Whatever I do must be profound if not popular. The subject is too critical for trivializing. It must be available for those who have a heart, a zeal for obedience. The very theme may *not* appeal to those pastors domesticated by the age of death.

This points again to an insistent question: Is it possible that in spite of the energy given to church structures, the church has lost sight of the true doorway? Has it forgotten the threshold of radical repentance and new obedience that gives access to the joyous news of this kingdom? Has the church failed to recognize the malignant character of this present age and conformed to it?

We have millions of church members, innumerable people in Sunday schools, tens of millions who profess to be born again, a great company who weekly partake of the bread and wine of the Lord's Supper. How can they still be so comfortable with the age of death? Why are the mandates of the Great King so rarely on our minds? Why have we created a church that lacks repentance, true faith, and kingdom integrity? Why have we fashioned, unintentionally and unobserved, a pastoral office that leads this community, unaware that it is betraying its calling?

This seems too cynical, too unlikely to be taken seriously. But let a pastor begin, ever so gently and lovingly, to call forth kingdom reality and kingdom obedience in one of these congregations, and all hell breaks loose. Members exchange intimidating, accusing, threatening words with the pastor and each other. Pastors face subtle discouragements and irrational emotional harassments.

Why?

Why is the reality of the dominion of Satan such a scandal to our theological schools? Why is the theology of the church so seldom dealt with in the context of its radical and eschatological otherness, its *called-out-ness*? Why are pastors marched out, master of divinity degrees in hand, ready for routine, as though there were no warfare to be fought with the prince of darkness?

You, dear pastoral brothers and sisters, sincere, believing, but ill-equipped to fight the spiritual battles in the heavenly places (Eph. 6:12)—you are my target audience. I hope you may awaken from the nightmare and become agents of the Messiah, who builds his church. I want to call you again to mirth, laughter, and joy amid conflict as you walk in harmony with the Vision. So be it! Lord, have mercy.

2

It's Not Neutral Out There

WE MET shortly after the conference—Seduction, Frustration, Resolution, and I. Their awakening to the fading of the Vision made them the more eager to reach out for hope and for understanding of what they were experiencing. Ben expressed it well: "We were all so naive. We assumed it would all be full of goodwill and productive work. We thought the setting would be neutral." What we seldom contemplate when we start out is what the psalmist experienced.

> The arrogant are attacking me, O God;
> a band of ruthless men seeks my life—
> men without regard for you. (Ps. 86:14)

In their mutual quest to recapture their Vision and integrity of calling, I heard a cry for a word of hope. They could have listened to many who speak gloom, but they invited me to join them. They did this not because of my great achievements or wisdom but because they knew I had struggled with the same issues of principle, of theology, and of integrity. So the request came: "Bob, we've told you our dismay. You've been there much longer than we have. Tell us how you've maintained your sense of spiritual and theological integrity through the years."

I put them in touch with one of my models, Francis of Assisi. In the dismal, drought-stricken ecclesiastical landscape of twelfth-century Italy, he appeared as one of God's choice gifts of renewal. He had an irrepressible spirit, so self-effacing, so devoted to his Lord Jesus. I love him as a model of life in the midst of death, of hope amid hopelessness. Francis sang the Lord's song in a weary land. He is one of those who, when passing "through the Valley of Baca, . . . make it a place of springs" (Ps. 84:6). He had eyes for the kingdom of God—and for the Great King.

Francis took the Sermon on the Mount literally! He was so genuine and eccentric that the church didn't know what to do with him. So he sang and preached and modeled the kingdom. Others gathered about him in his community of "friars minor." What happened? Rivers of living water flowed into parched ecclesiastical surroundings. I love the name given him: *le jongleur de Dieu*, the troubadour of God![1] However, he paid a price. Francis renounced the expectations of economic security, family, friends, church, and society—expectations that were alien to the Vision. In so doing, he became that instrument of joy.

In the vast, present wilderness of ecclesiastical and pastoral disillusionment, we desperately need troubadours of God. We need singers of the Lord's song, instruments of God's joy to model and to create communities that incarnate the new creation of God. What would it look like to have a new generation of such joyous troubadours in the wasteland which today so often passes for the kingdom?

Through Francis, I wanted to place at least one classic model before my friends. I needed to do this because I knew that some pastors are ready to succumb to self-pity, anger, depression, and escapism. We are tempted to pout in corners with our blankets and emotionally suck our thumbs. Other pastors are tempted to say, "What the heck!" (or something more colorful), and become religious lapdogs, adopting cultural values and currying the favor of those who provide our maintenance.

At the same time, apart from our own inner struggles, we are continually made aware that North America is a mission field. Surveys reveal that church folk are little different from the rest of society in values or behavior. Both church and culture are post-everything—post-Christian, post-modern, post-denominational. Hence, we have to recognize the cultural nighttime, darkness so thick it can be felt (Exod. 10:21). But it is even more ominous when the torchbearers themselves, who are to enlighten the community of the new creation, are swallowed up by the darkness (John 1:6; Eph. 5:8-14).

So we march forth from seminaries, having undergone what one witty observer called our "theological puberty rites." We are led to think that we have a lot to offer as shepherds of God's flock, teachers of the people of God, stewards of the divine mysteries, ministers of the Word of God and the table of the Lord, heralds of the joyous news of the kingdom of God. We think of congregations as warm, gentle, and responsive, waiting gratefully for our skills.

This illusion is given temporary substance in those initial days of ordination and in the warm congratulations and affirmations of friends, family, and congregation. The illusion can persist for weeks, months, even longer. Then comes *disillusionment*. The dream is shattered. The minions of darkness emerge. They appear in guises emotional, personal, societal, organizational, spiritual, or however. They inevitably emerge where least expected. They accuse, discourage, blight, and dare you to be faithful to the Vision.[2] Our adversary is clever. Lord, "deliver us from the evil one" (Matt. 6:13). I doubt that many persons begin pastoral ministry with much awareness of what hostility may await them.

I remember my own bitter taste of disillusionment. In seminary days my ego was enhanced by the applause of older leaders in my tradition. I thought I could do no wrong. The revival of the church awaited my arrival. What Goliaths of theological and ecclesiastical error were awaiting the well-aimed stones of this faithful David?

However, it wasn't such an expected Goliath who defied me (and the armies of God I thought I commanded). Instead, the illusion was pierced by the most vocal grande dame of this "tall steeple" congregation. She was a woman of wealth and social prominence, one who played a dominant role in the church and was the wife of an elder. This was an eagle-eyed champion of fundamentalist orthodoxy who could discover motes of false doctrine in the eyes of the straightest company of Puritans!

I walked right into her ambush. A few weeks earlier, I as associate pastor declined one of her proposals for my ministry. In so doing, I became "the enemy." She chose the battlefield and the moment of attack. The setting was a mellow Sunday afternoon in a well-appointed and musty-smelling church parlor during a regular meeting of the leadership council. The session opened with prayer and initial amenities. She began a forty-five minute, nonstop diatribe against me. The council and the senior pastor sat stunned, embarrassed, and confused as this prominent person accused me of being some sinister instrument of error in their midst, a "liberal," the worst thing to happen in that church. My illusion of a happy, accepting congregation was under fire. The warfare was real!

My role in that church was to minister to university students. It had been a thrilling time and a wonderful initiation into my disciple-making role. The community of students was keen and exciting. The New Testament message had come alive. Lives had been changed. Minds had come under the transforming effect of Scriptures. Vocational decisions had been made and careers launched under the touch of Jesus Christ. A community of the kingdom of God had been called forth with some biblical integrity and had produced some kingdom-shaped results.

In retrospect, I have to assume that the enemy was not about to let that happen unchallenged. In theory and through the ministry of Christian mentors, I knew about spiritual conflict. However, I was definitely not ready to be a target for the fiery darts of the wicked one, especially when the darts were real, verbal, and painful! What dismay, bruised ego, self-doubt, anger, and counter schemes! This experience gave me a generous introduction into the agony of disillusionment, where spiritual warfare is no mere theory and where darkness can be touched.

Does this sound familiar? "Deliver us from the evil one," we pray with our Lord Jesus.

A word from the apostolic writings gave light in my darkness.

> And the Lord's servant must not quarrel; instead, he must be kind to everyone, able to teach, not resentful. Those who oppose him he must gently instruct, in the hope that God will grant them repentance leading them to a knowledge of the truth, and that they will come to their senses and escape from the trap of the devil, who has taken them captive to do his will. (2 Tim. 2:24-26)

Those inspired words were stamped on my mind and burned into my heart. I have remembered them again and again as I have reacted in anger or self-pity to the darkness inside the church. The words remind us that there are tenured church members who are captive to darkness. Still, I was convinced at the time that the grande dame's attack must be an aberration, an unusual case of a neurotic zealot. My illusion was scratched but still basically intact.

My ordination followed. I moved into our denomination's campus ministry at a large land-grant university in the midfifties. Those where halcyon days of exciting interaction with the lively and inquiring minds of student visionaries. And I was one of them! Optimism, idealism—and unrealism.

That was when the World Council of Churches and the World Student Christian Federation were producing landmark works on the nature and mission of the church. There were books aplenty probing the whole subject of the church. Emil Brunner had written *Misunderstanding the Church*. John Robert Nelson was exploring *The Realm of Redemption*, and Lesslie Newbigen described *The Household of God*. Bonhoeffer's *Life Together* and *The Cost of Discipleship* were "in" books among my students.

We read, devoured, discussed, and debated them in the delicious detachment one enjoys only in that heady and adolescent university world. We saw the church in its "pure" divine intention (the illusion). Even such disturbing favorites of that generation as George Bernanos' *Diary of a Country Priest* and Trevor Huddleston's *Naught for Your Comfort* were products of another generation or at least half a world away. Yet, they did speak of loneliness, dismay, and forces of darkness and death that impinge on the local congregation (the disillusion).

The unwanted disillusionment was waiting just around the corner. All that theological study and discussion didn't prepare me for the assaults of "the death"—but it did give to me a clear sense of divine purpose for the community of faith. This Vision purpose must be noted here, since it will become a critical factor in the discussion which follows. But in so much of these writings, there was the nonbiblical assumption of the cultural setting and ethos as somehow neutral.

With this background, I took the next step in my pilgrimage. I was called to a barely alive community of faith, a dull-gray congregation surviving without hope. Its very building reinforced its poor self-image. A dirty red-brick structure of dubious architectural vintage, it was on a side street, in the shadow of a typical clattering southern cotton mill, though also in the neighborhood of a major university. Because of this period in my life, I can identify with Andy in his quest to minister to an industrial community and its particular social expressions.

I accepted the call in good faith, with my illusions and good theology intact. I was their fourth pastor in a five-year period; that says something in itself. Just as I arrived, the civil rights movement erupted in the nation, and particularly in that city. It was expressed there in the early lunch-counter demonstrations.

White folk were struggling for survival and meaning in a dismal textile community where racism was culturally entrenched. The prospect of equality in the work force was economically threatening. There was little joy in the Lord. Quite the opposite. The small faith in the congregation was mixed with fear, pettiness, and an unhappy tradition of traditional religion. These cultural facts are a clue. Hopelessness, negativity, suspicion, pettiness, and fear are part of the "dominion of darkness" (Col. 1:13), the age of death.

So this young visionary arrived in the bliss of illusion to deliver these unsuspecting folk. I did the right things. I faithfully taught and preached the Scripture. I sincerely wanted to know and love the congregation in which I was convinced God had called me to be pastor. I visited in homes. I cultivated the leadership. But I was suspect, respected at arm's length, a stranger—and lonely. I was a member of the larger presbytery and accountable to it, but that body was occupied with presbytery matters and had little interest in me.

Then I encountered the typical little blue-haired Jezebels and Ahabs in three-piece suits who inhabit too many churches. The *disillusionment* was no chilling plunge into a crisis. Instead, it was an elder in the church who took perverse delight in reporting to me what "everybody is saying." The anonymous everybodies were saying unflattering, negative, critical things—aimed at me. I learned to count noses, and I saw that these everybodies are usually a tiny group who reinforce each others' unhappiness.

Disillusionment was stirred by a pillar of the Ladies' Bible Class. She was a marvelously efficient information source. She challenged my sermons on kingdom integrity, including my teaching that there was no place for racial discrimination in the family of God.

Bible in hand, I paid her a visit. After the customary pleasantries, we got to the subject. I read 1 John 4:20 for her (pastors are supposed to read from the Bible, aren't they?) and posed the apostle John's question, "How then can we say we love God whom we have not seen, if we do not love our brother whom we have seen?" Lamely she assured me she "loved" them, but they had churches of their own, which was where they belonged.

I said it would be difficult for people to convince me that they really loved me if they didn't want me in their houses. "I don't care what the Bible says. I don't want those [unprintable] people in my church," she bitterly and loudly proclaimed.

The darkness had spoken. The light was challenged. The conflict was real, and conflict always comes when the gospel is proclaimed. It comes in different forms and in different milieus, but it is always there to challenge the light. So I identified with Debbie, Andy, and Ben.

Since then, I have often wondered what it would have been like if I had been called to pastoral ministry in the reign of Jeroboam II of Israel! In that period in the Northern Kingdom of Israel, the king, the priests, the nation, and the culture had all forsaken the covenant. How would a faithful pastor, with the heart of an Amos, have carried out responsibility to the Holy One of Israel? What kind of an eccentric would it take? Is it so different today? Is the world of darkness less pervasive now than it was in ancient Israel?

From where does this spiritual death come? Why so often from inside the congregation? Why at such strategic moments? In retrospect, I see that every time I or my congregations engaged in a major effort of Christian outreach or gospel obedience, there was an unexpected and destructive crisis.

Lest this all seem negative and ominous, I offer the other side. Such occasions were also breakthrough moments into new life and power for my congregations. In my first congregation, several African-American students joined the church. Nearly the whole company of those opposed to the kingdom agenda left. The elders were sensitive, compassionate, and determined to obey Christ.

From that moment, the congregation began a witness to the community, to the university, and ultimately to the world—a ministry which continues several decades later. But this was also the result of some internal disciplines, of implementing the pattern given on the mount, which we will discuss in a later chapter. Walking through conflict with the risen Christ gives mirth in the midst of pain. This is the one "who for the joy that was set before him endured the cross, scorning its shame" (Heb. 12:2).

• • •

I shared the above autobiographical thoughts with my three colleagues. In the years following these episodes, I have pastored churches both similar to and different from theirs. Yet the same darkness-and-light conflict has emerged in all of them.

Debbie broke in with a necessary question: "What is the difference between real and valid spiritual conflict over the gospel of God, and reaping the results of your own stupidity or ineptness?" We agreed that we needed to be reminded that such human stupidity was a possibility. Part of our ongoing discipline should be to refine the human skills necessary to avoid this. But we also faced the reality of another dimension of conflict which defies such easy explanation. We discussed the ambiguity of this relation between humanly caused conflict, and conflict that is spiritual at a different level or in a different dimension.

We pondered the need to remember that even if the dominion of Satan includes this world, ultimately "this is my Father's world." We keep in mind the *common grace*, God at work preserving creation and bringing about good things, even from people who do not acknowledge God's being.

We discussed the different expressions of the age of death. In addition to spiritual blindness, unbelief, and direct opposition, there is the "drag" factor, evident at those times when God's purposes seem to have the brakes on. There are those merely human failings which nevertheless contribute to a larger age of death. There are traditions which contradict or resist God's new creation. There are personalities who resist the Spirit and play by a different set of rules. There is the spirit of this disobedient age (Eph. 2:1-2) that contemporary scholars might call "the dominant social order" or the "plausibility structures" which determine the acceptable codes of thinking and behaving. There are those zeitgeists, those faddish spirits of the day that for a time dominate church and culture.

All four of us had been reading contemporary studies of the church adopting dominant cultural models of thinking and living. We were aware that much of our thinking has been molded by Christendom and the Enlightenment. Christendom made us think that all of the culture around us was congenial to the church. The Enlightenment taught us that religion was private and personal, not public. Both Christendom and the Enlightenment were wrong, but their influence over the church has made the church more vulnerable. We had assumed that conflict in a church would be fought by the rules of what is proper and genteel. Instead, the conflict is more like guerrilla warfare. It comes unseen from unexpected quarters and often from unknown causes and persons.[3]

However, God promises that somehow in our weakness and vulnerability, if we are faithful and rely on God's power, God will work out his ultimate good purpose in Christ. The dominion of God continues breaking into this world in spite of the evil one. Yes!

• • •

A clue in a footnote set off a chain reaction in my consciousness about the nature of pastoral ministry. It is in the quote which Andy shared in the discussions with Debbie and Ben. I reported it earlier. Overbeck contends that "all Christian theology" (and the church?) has since Patristic times been "unchristian and satanic, since it draws Christianity into the sphere of civilization and culture, and thereby denies the eschatological character of the Christian religion."[4]

Perhaps it is too much to ask that we evaluate the

church and its conflicts and pastoral traumas on the basis of a questionable quote from an obscure theologian (even if Karl Barth resurrected the quote with approval).

Or is it?

3

Achor and Hope: Caricature of Churches at the Poles

OUR NEXT time together was a day spent at a monastery. We pondered what a church that incarnated the integrity of the gospel of Christ might look like, and what one that did *not* live the gospel would look like. We projected two caricatures and named them so they could be points of reference in our pursuit of the Vision. We gave them names from a prophecy in Hosea: the *valley of Achor,* where Israel stoned Achan and his family for bringing defeat upon Israel (Josh. 7); and a *door of hope,* which Yahweh promised to create in the middle of that cursed place. "There I will give her back her vineyards, and will make the Valley of Achor a door of hope" (Hos. 2:15).

Our fabricated congregations exemplify opposite poles in this discussion.[1] The *Valley of Achor Church*[2] has familiar trappings, including buildings, hymnbooks, clergy, organization, tenured members, budget, and tradition. Through its relationship with the larger tradition, it has a constitution and a formal theology, a heritage that is a commendable witness to the light.

Like the church at Sardis (Rev. 3:1-6), it has a reputation of being alive. It receives members and loses some. It conducts services it calls "worship." It observes the sacraments. But somehow it is all so arid; so much an episode of religious death; so devoid of any hearty sense of faith, love, living hope. Members are accepted and leaders elected because they enhance the institution, not because they meet standards of faith in Christ or of discipleship. There are few, if any, conversions in which persons come to new faith in Christ and have visibly changed lives. Polite scorn greets any suggestion that this state of affairs be changed.

One is overwhelmed with the sense that there is no robust repentance, no sense of calling from darkness to light, no *alternative consciousness*,[3] no informing or compelling awareness of being the unique community of the dominion of God, a new humanity in Christ. Certainly there is no understanding of the "eschatological character of the Christian religion."[4]

"The Death" becomes acceptable; this borrowed term defines life apart from the radical newness which comes through salvation in Christ. The great joy and the "sheer spiritual zest of New Testament Christianity"[5] is missing. There are remnants of gospel memory, of patient and faithful folk who pray and wait quietly for the visitation of the Spirit. But mostly, joy is missing and the lack appears normal. Nobody seems alarmed that the congregation offers only human religion carried on decently and in order! The legacy of darkness is acceptable and expected, a legacy of discouragement, of leadership inhabiting spiritual death. The wineskin itself and not the new wine of the gospel is their reason for being. This sophisticated and sterile community is the Valley of Achor Church.

Its imaginary counterpart, the *Door of Hope Church,*

seems outwardly similar. Its buildings and organization are not that different from its sister church. But the Door of Hope Church is tangibly alive and expectant. There is the fragrance of life (2 Cor. 2:14-16). Jesus Christ is the most obvious reality in this church. His identity, teaching, life, and requirements for discipleship are most important. Jesus affects who is received into membership, who leads, how the congregation's life is formed, and where its corporate resources are focused. This church has a sense of calling that motivates it toward costly discipleship. It is dynamic but without fanfare. "Peace and joy and justice in the Holy Spirit" (Rom. 14:17) might describe its life together. Members express real bonding love and a spirit of praise and worship, without affected airs.

Door of Hope is a contagious congregation. People regularly come to faith in Christ. They are set free and changed by the power of God in the gospel. The word of the Lord and the Spirit of the Lord are assumed presences. People outside the congregation notice and talk about the congregation's kingdom behavior. Door of Hope expresses the compassion of Christ in many spontaneous ways. At the same time, it is human and shares in the pain, failures, and lapses of any congregation. It is alive!

Two congregations so alike—yet so different.

• • •

My three friends said that they could identify pieces of each caricature in their own congregations. Remember that the caricatures are exactly that. No congregation is totally one or the other. Each caricature gives us an image of the difference between life and death, the dominion of God and the dominion of Satan. Behavior in the congregation originates, not in a neutral zone, but under the dominion of God or the dominion of Satan.

Ben was sobered. "That Achor caricature is almost normative in the churches I know. Now that you describe it, I see that it's like mine. How do we lose the Vision without noticing what has happened? Is that a normal state of affairs in the church?"

• • •

Why does this happen in churches? How do we account for this?

Try our "Overbeck Principle." One congregation forgets or is oblivious to its *eschatological* calling. The other is conscious of its calling to be the community of the age to come. Both are made up of fallible, sinful humans who profess the grace of God in Jesus Christ.

One is content to be the religious community of the age of death. The other lives with the expectation and empowering of the age of life and light, the kingdom of God. One has been blinded and taken captive by "the prince of this world" (John 12:31). Religion, not Christ, is the focus of its corporate life. Loyalty to the institution (or the denomination) is its central concern.

The other, by the power of God's keeping grace, sees Jesus (Heb. 2:9). This church sees that Jesus invades this age and calls out a people to build his church, against which the gates of the death and hell cannot prevail (Matt. 16:18).

So alike. So different.

Ah, but there's the rub! What if our visionary young pastor believes the congregation is a community like Door of Hope? What if she assumes it will live up to the name, will, and reign of God? What if this pastor assumes that the cultural-social context of such a pastoral ministry is neutral or even congenial to the gospel? Take note!

If that parish is a Valley of Achor and the new pastor

comes with a kingdom agenda, then darkness does not passively accept this intrusion of light. "For look, the wicked bend their bows; they set their arrows against the strings to shoot from the shadows at the upright in heart" (Ps. 11:2).

The pastor may have sincere and genuine intentions and kingdom integrity. But in spite of all that, opposition (sophisticated or blatant) will come; bleak days and the satanic *skubalon* (rubbish)[6] will come flying "from the shadows." There will be in-house persecutions, psychological brutality, subtle intimidation, and economic control. Some will use the pastor's "divine calling" to insist that he or she must passively accept pastor-abuse. There will be satanic opposition—demonic, irrational, destructive, unwarranted.

My friends began to compare notes. "At first the intimidations are polite, with a chuckle, a pat on the back, and a sweet encouragement to back off or your popularity might take a hit," said Andy.

"Yeah!" Ben exclaimed. "Right when I'm about to tee off on the fourth hole, a snide suggestion. Ouch! But even more distressing is how often I am tempted to leave out or mute some demanding parts of Scripture so I won't upset anyone—almost weekly."

Debbie's lament was of a different genre. She struggled with heavy pressures to adopt programs and materials from the denomination or from other sources. Yet some of these proposals did not fit her congregation and had little to do with Scripture. She felt compromised if she gave in, yet felt some sense of responsibility and accountability to the denominational resources.

If the pastor gives a sound message, another evil strategy is to discredit the messenger. Gifted pastors go down in flames because their characters are unjustly impugned. They grapple with onslaughts of depression because of the fiery darts from Satan, the accuser, the destroyer.

Sometimes I think I would like to trade places with Fr. Jerzey Popieluszko, priest and chaplain to the Polish Solidarity movement in its early days. He was beaten to death one night by government police. I would rather be Archbishop Romero, martyred by a single shot in the back while standing at the altar in El Salvador. I would almost rather suffer one death than the wearying, eroding weeks and months of anonymous pressure, gossip, networks of malice behind smiling faces, emotional brutality, and discouragements.

One morning I read, in the same journal, accounts of Fr. Miguel D'Escoto in Nicaragua, of Archbishop Desmond Tutu of South Africa, and of the faithful church in Burundi—all undergoing severe repression. These are dramatic, heroic, faithful, heartening, and terrifying episodes of the clash of evil and God's love in turbulent nations.

Look at the pastor of the Valley of Achor Church. His self-pity has cause, as he faces the subtle accusations and mean remarks uttered by members with smiling faces. Then add the burdens of financial hopelessness (as often with Andy) or the seductions of financial prosperity (as with Ben). All of this melts the heart right out of the well-intentioned visionary, the gifted but naive young pastor, who soon, like Annie Dillard's frog, is sucked dry by the giant waterbug.

Debbie couldn't contain herself at this point. "You bet. We do get our guts sucked out, and all the while denominational committees drearily debate the need for evangelism or trumpet some messianic new program which will solve all our problems. Groan."

"I deliberately want to use the word *demonic* with you," I responded. "I do believe there is a destructive energy at work to drain the church of obedience to Jesus

Christ. But though there are times when there is public, political, and external violence, most of what you will experience is not brazen and grotesque stuff. It will more often be subtle, distracting, or subversive. It may come through malicious attacks on your ministry by folk who totally dislike you. It may come as pious suggestions from close friends who lead you away from the purpose of God. But note, it will usually come from *inside* the Christian community. It is always more painful to be attacked or seduced from inside than from outside."

Still, if I am the pastor of the dismaying Valley of Achor Church, self-pity is not a redemptive response. It may be justified, perhaps, but it is not redemptive. How do I discern the engagement of good and evil in this community? It has, indeed, a "form of godliness" (2 Tim. 3:5), but the evil is so real that I wonder if God has abandoned me here. Are the powers of the age to come able to bring joy, life, light, and salvation into this "religion"? What happens when I am seduced into a passive role, simply engaging in the responsibilities of church professionals that have little to do with the mission of God? How does that happen?

Congregations are seldom what they seem to be at first. They have a public face and an inner reality. It is too easy, like Elijah, to lament, "I am the only one left" (1 Kings 19:10, 14), and not to discern God's purpose, the Spirit's vessels, or the hand and power of God.

Ask the questions: How did this evil come about? What is the source of the mistrust? Is there reason for members to be suspicious of pastors? What is it? Has the fellowship endured betrayal by a former pastor? How has this community been used by pastors to enhance their own careers? What blighted self-image cloaks itself with angry pride?

On the other hand, who are the quiet ones in the congregation who walk with God and pray? They are often out of sight, silent, and non-assertive—just faithful. Who are the real conductors of God's power into this community?

• • •

"I know what you're going to ask. Okay, if no one else is available to conduct God's power, are we the conductors? Right?" Andy asked. "But I'm getting nervous with where you're going. You're suggesting a *demonic* factor. Hey! That ain't too popular, you know."

No, it isn't the hottest theological item on the scene. But look carefully at Scripture; demythologize it all you want. There remains a battle behind the battle, a consciousness, another dimension of pastoral and ecclesiastical reality that must be faced. If there is not an energizing demonic reality, then the gospel enterprise should go uphill, faith should produce more faith, and obedience and worship should increase in quantum leaps with each new generation of faith. But that is not what is happening. Later-generation church members often are less formed by the faith of Jesus Christ than their first-generation parents or grandparents.

Before we can approach these examples of death and life (the Achor and Hope churches), we need to come to terms with the reasons for the attacks. If the motives are only human, that's one thing. But if there is a battle behind the battle, then we will not serve ourselves or God well by copping out simply because "it ain't popular."

"Whoa!" Debbie chimed in. "I've got a problem with the idea that my friends and members who grump, discourage others, and behave in lousy ways are in some way part of the demonic. Hey! Everybody wakes up on the wrong side of the bed some days. Explain!"

I responded that, yes, suggesting demonic causes

does seem a bit much. Then again, we need to look at the source of behavior. We think humanity is basically neutral or that the normal is good. We write off aberrations with inane comments: "Nobody's perfect all the time." But biblically, there are two dominions or ages. There is this satanic age, and there is God's age, the age to come. The one is this creation in its fallen state, things going on as usual. The other is the new creation that broke in at the coming of Jesus. The people with whom we deal reflect one or the other.

We think everybody is basically good. The demonic is out there in some bizarre fashion on one pole; Spirit-filled people are out there on the other pole. Meanwhile, most of us just muddle along happily in some neutral zone between these extremes.

That may be our perception, but it is not the biblical picture. This age is dominated by the discouraging, the demeaning, the destructive, the selfish, and the dehumanizing. God's mercy expressed in common (or preserving) grace prevents creation's self-destruction and produces the good despite rebellion. If you are thinking biblically, you know that lousy, demeaning behavior "is earthly, unspiritual, of the devil," while "the wisdom that comes down from heaven is first of all pure, then peaceloving, considerate, submissive, full of mercy and good fruit, impartial and sincere" (James 3:15, 17).

Our congregations exist in the battlefield of the ages, on contested ground, driven by the fallenness of the old age *and* by the new set of redemptive principles rooted in the coming of Jesus Christ, the dawning age.[7] No congregation is completely Valley of Achor or Door of Hope. We pastors are always *evangelizing* congregations into newness by the power of the Spirit, by the powers of the age to come. Yet this present evil age, this dominant social order, continually expresses itself in the congregation.

We need to look afresh at our identity with Jesus and his mission. We are called to see and do what Jesus (and the apostles) saw and did. This is incarnation. This is creating communities of God in the midst of the evil. Our task is to act like Jesus did and always to herald the joyous good news of God even while surrounded by joyless self-actualization, cynicism, and hopeless hyperactivity. If we suffer in the process, Jesus welcomes us into his sufferings and also into his joy.

• • •

As cultural darkness manifests itself in North America and increasingly infiltrates the church, it will become more difficult to be a pastor faithful to the gospel of the reign of God. Pastors will be tempted to engage in *elision*,[8] to omit from the New Testament message what is not acceptable to the dominant social order. Pastors will be seduced into making the church more marketable to the neo-pagan populace. As these moves become more common, the reduction will hardly be noticed. This is happening in all segments of the church, evangelical and ecumenical. A subtle seduction subverts the gospel into a religion which is comfortable with the culture of hedonism, consumerism, and self-actualization.

• • •

That is why we must pursue the church as a different or *eschatological* community of pilgrims and strangers who have entered the threshold of repentance, then the door of faith. The four of us processed such issues briefly. Then we agreed we needed to work on an *ecclesiology*, a theology of the church, in light of the biblical concept of clashing dominions.

4

The Community of the Great King: An Ecclesiology

SEVERAL WEEKS later the four of us met again at the monastery. We had many unanswered questions, but we agreed on this: We had *a Vision of the gospel and the church which was part and parcel of the joyous news of the kingdom of God.* The Vision, however, kept getting lost as we did what was expected of us as pastors.

Ben was eager to pursue the Vision. We could see his juices flowing. "Hey, guys, I'm getting a clue here that has me on tiptoes. I really love my church, though it has too much of an Achor profile. But I'm eager to know what it would take to see the new creation expressed in all of those crazy people I pastor."

Andy called us again to Overbeck's observation and said, "Let's get on with discovering the *eschatological* ecclesiology." So we reflected on the theology behind the Valley of Achor and the Door of Hope.

• • •

What does the Door of Hope Church see that Valley of Achor doesn't see?

> After John was put in prison, Jesus went into Galilee, proclaiming the good news of God. "The time has come," he said. "The kingdom of God is near. Repent and believe the good news!" (Mark 1:14-15)

When the Great King from heaven came, shared our humanity, and invaded our history, he issued an ecstatic announcement: The expected *malkuth shamayim*[1] (kingdom of heaven) is at the doorstep, the reign of God is upon you, the age to come has dawned! This is sheer joy! It is good news because the Great King is the sovereign Creator, gracious and merciful, slow to anger, and full of steadfast love. He is the Shepherd of Israel, faithful and compassionate, guarding his flock, and keeping them in his care.

But don't misunderstand the message. *He is the Great King!*

> Wonderful Counselor, Mighty God, Everlasting Father, Prince of Peace. Of the increase of his government and peace there will be no end. He will reign on David's throne and over his kingdom, establishing and upholding it with justice and righteousness from that time on and forever. The zeal of the Lord Almighty will accomplish this.
>
> (Isa. 9:6-7)

Don't misunderstand the message! The news is *good* precisely because of the holy name of God, the dominion of God, and the will of God. The news is good because of who God is and what God will irresistibly accomplish in the midst of this "people walking in darkness."

The Great King comes into this joyous dominion of God, this reign of grace, this establishing of justice and righteousness, this invasion of salvation, this coming of light and hope, this government that will be good news to the crushed and oppressed. The King calls out a people to be the Community of the Great King, with all of the redemptive reality defined by being part of his dominion.

However, don't misunderstand the message. There is a price to pay to enter the community: "Repent and believe the joyous news!" This call is no trivial exercise of piety. It is a totalitarian claim, a command to become a living member in the agenda of the holy God who calls! The holy God calls us to demonstrate his new creation, "that you may declare the praises of him who calls you out of darkness and into his wonderful light" (1 Pet. 2:9).

This is a call to otherness, to be "a cognitive deviant minority,"[2] to an "alternative consciousness,"[3] to be "the hermeneutic of the gospel,"[4] to be "resident aliens,"[5] to be salt and light, to be peculiar, and to belong to the Great King. The great joy is that we are his! That his grace and peace are multiplied to us! Don't misunderstand the message!

Jesus came preaching the kingdom of God. That was his message. Translate it anyway you will—the reign or dominion of God, of salvation, of righteousness, of the gospel, of eternal life, or of new creation. They are all related; all point toward the same reality. At Caesarea Philippi (Matt. 16:13-19), Jesus asked, "Who do you say I am?" Peter replied, "You are the Messiah, the Great King."

We must not misunderstand Jesus' next announcement: "On this rock I will build my church." I will call forth a people, a community to embody my name, to incarnate my will, to interpret my kingdom and my salvation! The gates of death and hell will not prevail against this new people founded on the rock of Jesus.

This is what the Door of Hope Church remembers and what Valley of Achor Church has forgotten. It is so easy to trivialize the calling, to reduce it to traditional religion, to emasculate its radical demands. Like the rescued Israelites in the wilderness, we quickly forget. We share with them the backward look, the security of slave quarters, and the certainty of the leeks and garlic of the dominant social order. Jealousy, unbelief, murmuring, conflicts—and the Passover fades to the periphery of the memory.

While we are being "very religious" (Acts 17:22), we easily allow "Christ, our Passover lamb" (1 Cor. 5:7), to fade from our mind, even as we seem to be highly religious. Salvation, the calling by the Great King, does not summon us out of neutrality and into religion. Instead, it calls us out of one dominion and into another!

> I am sending you to them to open their eyes and turn them from darkness to light, and from the power of Satan to God. (Acts 26:17-18a)

We are delivered from an alien realm, from wrath, from evil. God the Father

> has rescued us from the power of darkness and transferred us into the kingdom of his beloved Son, in whom we have redemption, the forgiveness of sins. (Col. 1:13, NRSV)

We are called to a *new slavery,* a slavery to righteousness. Such a calling is a deliberate transfer of loyalties. It is a gracious summons to forsake a slavery to moral and spiritual darkness and death; a slavery to the merely human, the autonomous, the insensitive, the destructive, and the unrighteous—a slavery to sin.

> Don't you know that when you offer yourselves to someone to obey him as slaves, you are slaves to the one whom you obey—whether you are slaves to sin, which leads to death, or to obedience, which leads to righteousness? But thanks be to God that, though you used to be slaves to sin, you wholeheartedly obeyed the form of teaching to which you were entrusted. You have been set free from sin and have become slaves to righteousness. (Rom. 6:16-18)

No casual church membership here! That is exactly Overbeck's point. We have reduced the inbreaking dominion of God to a pious community congenial with the age of death. The church in the Valley of Achor is embarrassed when God says, "Repent and believe the joyous news." Repentance is strong, deliberate, hearty, and intentional. Repentance is the consciously chosen death to all of the crude or sophisticated rebellion stirred up by Satan!

• • •

Debbie, our liturgist, said, "I haven't heard that word very often: *repentance*. Even in the liturgical confessions, we confess and are forgiven, even though there has been no encouragement to repent, much less a command to do so. Interesting!"

• • •

Believe the good news! Yes! That wild and free embracing of the Great King. Wholehearted slavery to him who forgives and frees and transforms us into his likeness and binds us to himself in love and holiness. This calling, the most obvious of all, is what has been forgotten by one church and remembered by another. But in Scripture such good news always begins with *repentance.*

It is too easy to suggest that one church is secure and

the other is in peril. The evil can intrude unnoticeably. In the ordinary and the routine, the evangel is displaced. The sense of identity and vocation are muted. The wineskin becomes its own reason for being, rather than becoming the vessel for the new wine of the gospel (Mark 2:22). Jesus and the kingdom are obscured inside the church.

"Show me Christ in Christendom!"[6]

How does it happen? I was walking in a picturesque German village on a Sunday morning. The Evangelical Church stood on a hilltop at the center of town. According to the bronze plaque on the wall, Reformation witness had established a congregation in the sixteenth century. This building was erected in the seventeenth century. But on that Sabbath, a tiny remnant gathered for worship services. The light of God burns dimly. Why? Why are Germany and much of the West now mission fields? Or have they always been?

The downward slope from faith to faithlessness is slippery. So is the reversion into darkness. Seduction can come through a building program, a church-growth seminar, a zeal for organization, the temptations of wealth and influence, a zeal to preserve the traditions of the past, a bondage to patterns of order useful in generations gone by, success, or social acceptance. For the first generation, faith in Christ is dynamic and full of joy. For the second generation, it is important but not quite so precious. For the third and fourth generations, it is all a tradition, rites with which they have lived, rites important to parents but no longer significant for the children.

Lead us not into temptation!

The Valley of Achor Church is like a rare work of art which time and neglect and well-meaning people have buried under layers of lesser paintings. The glorious gospel of Christ is obscured but is still there. The name of Father, Son, and Holy Spirit is upon it. It is a relic of what points ultimately to Jesus and the cross. The Scripture, the hymns, the traditions, and the mindlessly performed rites —all point to a treasure hidden there somewhere.

• • •

"Yeah! Are you giving me the hope that no matter how dim the gospel burns in an Achor, somehow it is still the church?" Ben asked. He wondered how his big, successful congregation could break out into newness and into some integrity in accord with Vision and not be written off. I affirmed his search, but noted that it would require much faith and patience.

• • •

However Achor became what it is; whatever its poor foundations of wood, hay, and stubble; whatever corporate decisions led to unbelief and disobedience; whatever the erosions of time and forgetfulness—God is the one who grieves and weeps most. He calls and is merciful. The ascended Lord patiently invites, "He who has an ear, let him hear what the Spirit says" (Rev. 2:7). The Lord calls the church to repentance and faith; the Lord can make a Door of Hope in the Valley of Achor (Hos. 2:15).

• • •

Andy was struggling. "I have often wondered if I might land in some kind of ideal Door of Hope church. I've often wanted just to run away. Is there a time to shake the dust off your feet, when everything is so dismal and everyone so unbelieving? Someone might ask, Who will stand forth to be God's agent, to call back, to restore, to evangelize these Valley of Achor congregations? Then I have to ask, How in the world is it done?

"I'm not sure I'm mature enough in my gospel formation and confidence in the inbreaking kingdom of God to hang in there endlessly. At the same time, I know God is at work. I do want to have such zeal for God's name and glory in the church that I will be available for such a task. It's tough for me. Still, I remember Jesus' confidence that his Father was working and that he was doing the Father's works. Too often I forget that and think I'm on my own. I'm in trouble. Lord, have mercy!"

• • •

Who will go to the mission field of the many Achor congregations? Let's name the agents of the kingdom. Those who evangelize the church, the community of the Great King, are *kingdom pastors*! We need a new genre of faithful pastor-teachers who are self-consciously of the age to come. Above all else, they must be faithful to Christ and his church. They must have eyes anointed to see the conflict between evil and good inside the family of God.

When kingdom pastors look at the most dysfunctional and diseased congregation, by faith they see beneath the discouraging present to the coming glory of God. They see the alien presence of religious death, of Satan's blighting breath. But they are persuaded that in such unlikely wildernesses, God shows forth his glory by breathing life into the Valley of Dry Bones and creating all things new.

• • •

That obviously didn't fit Debbie's idea of what fruitful pastoral ministry was all about. She looked me in the eye, and said, "I don't want to be thought a cynic, but I think you're a dreamer. What assurance can you give that there's any future in what you're proposing? It sounds good, and

I'm listening. But right now my confidence in my congregation is shaken."

"Debbie," I responded, "I *am* a dreamer. Every pastor is a dreamer, only some dream without an ecclesiology or a hope. If we pastors have eyes for God's missionary purpose in this North American mission field, we cannot accept a status-quo view of the church. There is a sense in which every congregation must be continually re-evangelized and each new generation called into God's mission—intentionally, aggressively, and creatively."

• • •

If Christ really is building his church, institutional maintenance is not an acceptable corporate principle. Those who have a kingdom ecclesiology are always looking at church and culture through the spectacles of Scripture, and always with missionary eyes, to discern how a particular congregation is carrying out that missionary calling.

The Lord who calls us to be his church and his pastors sends us with these words: "As the Father has sent me, I am sending you" (John 20:21). Our God-given calling and task in these congregations is to form kingdom-shaped missionary communities, which in turn become transforming communities.

If the Great King is not with us, our calling is hopeless. We have every right to be cynical and despairing. But if he is with us, pastoring becomes high adventure. If God is with us, and if we are identified with him in the cross and resurrection of Jesus Christ, we are not engaged in a triumphalist charade but in a walk of quiet integrity and faith.

The calling to be kingdom pastors is always visionary, but we also live with the promise,

> Now to him who is able to do immeasurably more than all we ask or imagine, according to his power that is at work within us, to him be glory in the church and in Christ Jesus throughout all generations, for ever and ever! Amen.
>
> (Eph. 3:20-21)

• • •

I told my three friends that the fact that the risen Lord walks with us makes our journey especially adventuresome and often foils our human ambitions. In the middle of my own formation and pain, when I was tempted to seek escape, the Lord gave me a poetic prayer which I still have on the wall. It helped me through a lot of bleak days.

It is the Lord of the harvest
  who calls me to harvest.
The vineyards belong to him,
  and he knows where I am.
This field may not be as large and fruitful
  as some others he owns,
But he requires his laborers to obey him,
  to abide in him,
  and to be faithful to him,
  not to rush to and fro
  seeking some great work to do.
Because I seek his face,
  I labor, toil, and strive.
Where the work is barren and fruitless,
  I must dig and dung it,
  but not condemn it.
It is, after all, not my work
  but me whom the Lord loves,
  and it is not my work that I serve,
  but the Lord.
My labors are but the continuation
  of my devotions.

"I think it's beginning to come through," Ben said. "This opens a lot of windows for me. I could even get excited. But, Bob, are you going to leave us here, or is there practical stuff in this battle behind the battle that we need to download?"

I assured them that the Vision was just the first step in the battle. The ongoing conflict is in implementing kingdom reality. We'd begin on that next time around. We prayed together about what we'd been working on. With hugs and blessings, we went our separate ways.

5

The Pattern Given on the Mount: Forming the Vision

IN THE WEEKS before we got together again at Andy's place, we had time to ponder the Vision. When gathered, we shared the realities of our lives and congregations, and the pastoral ministries which we offered to God in priestly sacrifice.

We kept struggling with *the question* of how and why congregations become so sterile. Ben, with cryptic laughter, said, "Yeah, who needs it?" Yet we were talking about real people, folks we dealt with and knew and loved.

"What do these people think? What do they expect from the church?" Andy asked.

"But more to the point, Bob," Debbie carried on, "how can I and how can we be instrumental in generating faith and love and hope? Where do we begin?"

Such responses are typical. Our quest, giving real form to the Vision, has to begin with Jesus. In John's Gospel it is clear that from the outset, Jesus faced the hostility of the Jerusalem establishment in all its religious, economic, and political dimensions. Through it all, Jesus maintained marvelous clarity of person and purpose. With candor he stated that he was not there on his own but that he had come from the Father, to do the work of the Father, and to speak the words of the Father. Wow! He had his mission from God the Father, and that formed all he did. That enabled him to see beyond the immediate to the ultimate—beyond the *skubalon* (rubbish).

Consider what a travesty it would be if we pastors attended the institutes on pastoral and congregational care and had good skills—but had no vision. Suppose the pastor had no dynamic sense of repentance toward God, no faith in Jesus Christ that converts and forms the pastor's life into the new creation, into the image of Christ. What might be expected from such a leader and the church pastored? It might be an interesting facsimile of a church, but the basic spiritual formation which makes the pastor and the church viable would be missing.

I remember when I, a card-carrying Protestant, listened to a renowned Roman Catholic archbishop at a pastors' conference. He reported that in his tradition he spent an hour each morning before the holy sacrament, before the body and blood of Christ, in communion with the Lord. He made the point that it was this communion with his Lord Jesus Christ that gave him authority and authenticity and made people listen to him. Such a critical point! We must live in Christ and have Christ's word live in us, so what we do is formed by who he is and what he came to do.

When the centrality of Christ and his God-given mission is marginalized, people identify with the church for the wrong reasons. They bring their alien ideologies with them. The gospel of the kingdom hardly touches them. Instead, their lives are basically shaped by ideologies of pleasure, security, religious aesthetics, nation, economy, and conservative or liberal causes. A basic discipline for the kingdom pastor is dwelling deeply in Christ, so life, thought, behavior, and vision flow from that relationship. Out of that will come the Vision.

This is God's Vision for the world. I have not walked toward the Vision alone. One of God's rich blessings as a pastor has been beautiful and mutually beneficial friendships with pastors and priests from many Christian traditions and from many nations. As we share with each other, our experiences seem more common than different.

When I told my friends this, Debbie exclaimed, "Bob, why don't you get to the point? You've told us about your successes and failures. But what principles helped you grasp the Vision?"

I received little help with conflict or renewal in my own seminary training. The focus was not on the church as conceived in the mission of God; perhaps that is a satanic ploy against the redemptive plan of God.

Two events catalyzed my quest for answers. Both were unexpected providences, and I believe both grew out of prayers for clarity of vision. First, I was invited to a seminary for two weeks of guided study in any field of my choosing. They sent a list of suggested study areas. I was overwhelmed with congregational organization that didn't work. I was frustrated with all the committees and structures others told me I ought to have. I was beset with guilt at all that was undone. I was tired and on the edge of depression. Discouragement harbored by key members of the congregation didn't help either. Could it change? How?

From my father, a professional engineer, I probably inherited a lot of pragmatism. I also have a stubborn streak of kingdom integrity which requires that what I and the church do should have some relation to what Christ intends. I asked to work in the philosophy of church administration. The seminary didn't understand the request. Church administration was just that: church administration. The church institution had to be administered. The library was well stocked with how-to books. That was the assumed direction.[1]

I explained to the professor assigned to me that I wasn't interested in the gimmicky how-to stuff. I wanted to know *why* we did all of the busy stuff. What did it have to do with what God wanted and had called his church to be and do? What was the purpose of church administration? Where did I, as pastor and teacher, fit that purpose? The professor thought it was a novel and impractical approach. Shaking his head, he turned me loose in the seminary library.

I browsed through stacks of books and magazines that promised to give answers, only to be disappointed time and again. There was lots of good stuff on how to be successful, capable, and efficient in maintaining one's professional role. All of it assumed good will and a mutually understood mission in congregations. Finally, by accident I found a couple of volumes on corporate management for the business sector. I'll always wonder how they turned up in a seminary library. Eureka! Two basic principles linger with me many years later. They have gotten me into trouble, too.

1. Management-executives of any corporate structure must have a lucid grasp of the corporate principle—the exact reason that the corporation exists. Then everything that takes place in the corporation must be measured against how it contributes to the realization of that corporate principle.

2. Any person or factor in the corporation that uses the resources of the corporation without contributing to the purpose of the corporation must be removed. This

calls for unrelenting honesty. Noncontributing policies, personnel, traditions, whatever—get rid of them!

There was more, but my mind latched onto those two principles. I began to relate them to who I was, where I was, and what Christ wanted his people to be and do in this world. I decided that people do a lot of busywork under the assumption that they're serving God. Such work consumes time and energy and produces zip!

Debbie shouted, "Amen to that! I sit on denominational committees with a lot of sincere people who spend untold hours 'serving,' and for what? Institutional loyalties are nurtured, but so little related to the gospel is accomplished."

All I needed now was the Lord's *corporate principle.*

In that same time period, I read one book by an Indian Christian and one by a Chinese Christian.[2] Both came from independent church traditions, but both were architects of fruitful indigenous Christian communities. Both frequently quoted this Hebrews 8:5 (and Exod. 25:40) passage: "See to it that you make everything according to the pattern shown you on the mountain."

This is the principle of my own tradition: "Ecclesia reformata, semper reformanda" (the church reformed, and always being reformed).

All the same, the simple, graphic biblical figure from the Mt. Sinai episode came with freshness to me. Exodus refers primarily to the building of the tabernacle: everything according to divine plan, everything with purpose, everything focused on God's place of meeting with his people. The marvelous author of Hebrews applies this pattern imagery to the life and worship of the community of the new and everlasting covenant focused in Christ.

The refreshing insight of the Chinese and the Indian church architects was that the Western churches added so many trappings to the church that God's design and purpose and maybe even God's message were obscured. Hence, they and their followers rejected the ecclesiastical wineskins that came with the Western missionaries in favor of a simpler and more indigenous and biblical design for the church. My Western pride and theological scholasticism were offended by some of their conclusions. But they understood the corporate principle, the biblical vision of the church. They had made exceptional contributions to gospel outreach.

Any kingdom pastor faces several questions:

1. Do I have a clear grasp of God's revealed pattern and purpose for this congregation, the pattern given on the mount? Do I have a vision of God's purpose for calling a people such as this?

2. Can I relate that pattern to the realities, confusion, and lack of Vision of the congregation I pastor? How does the pattern intersect with its corporate personality, leadership, denomination, and tradition?

3. Is the Vision sufficiently established in my consciousness as a master plan so I can be a transforming pastor, helping to move the congregation to some semblance of the pattern given on the mount? Does the *immediate* situation overwhelm the Vision?

4. Do I have a reasonable perception of the pathologies that have subverted Christ's purpose for this congregation?

5. Am I available enough, flexible enough, patient enough, and faithful enough? Am I marked by the cross, to walk with and evangelize[3] this people into this Vision?

"Hey!" Debbie exclaimed. "There are some prior questions I'd like to have answered. Who and why am I? Why am I here? Do I know what to do? Is this congregation viable? Is the risen Lord with me in this? Where is the 'whited harvest field' of which Jesus spoke, beyond the maintenance of this mostly visionless congregation?"

"Yes," I said, "add those good questions to the list."

The New Testament says the gift of pastor-teacher (the kingdom pastor) is given to the church to equip God's people for ministry (Eph. 4:11-13). Since this is true, then of all people, the pastor-teacher[4] needs to have a lucid grasp of God's dynamic purpose for the church. The kingdom pastor must always have in mind the irreducible Christian message. Most of all, she or he must be shaped by the pattern given on the mount and not wander mindlessly into a pernicious temptation toward clergy busywork. We need to see the church as it is without being appalled, depressed, or overwhelmed. We need to know the plan and disciplines that will move us from where we are toward where God wants us to be—and be thrilled with the prospect!

For some pastors and churches, such a concept may not make sense. There are super-pastors of super-churches or missionary fellowships who do have a vision of what they are about. But most pastors are involved with ordinary churches. These are second- or third-generation (or later) congregations that have often forgotten their roots.[5] Such congregations are the majority; you won't read thrilling accounts about them in church journals. We pastors will find people in various stages of faith (or lack of it). We will deal with buildings, history, traditions, and organizations already in place, mixing darkness and light. Some members are more concerned to protect their own investments in all this than to serve God's reign.

It probably is not productive to ask Valley of Achor churches what their vision is or whether they want change, awakening, or renewal. It is unlikely they will give more than a polite response to a challenge to make a new start. They probably would have little idea what you were talking about, no biblical image in mind.

If you read the usual congregational information or

mission forms, you will see that most congregations have survival goals rather than mission goals; or they have institutional goals, not kingdom goals. They might be thinking: Well, it can't get any worse, so any change will be for the better. Some members jump enthusiastically on any new program. But they do so only until it begins to cost them. Meanwhile, the rest will protest:

- What's wrong with the way we are?
- What did you have in mind?
- That's never been done here.
- Are you suggesting that you don't approve of us or of the way we do things?
- Oh, yes! If we could just be like we were in the 1950s again. Those were good years.
- Why do you ask?
- Preacher, this church sure does need a great revival.
- Yes, if we only had more members, we could have a bigger budget and renovate our facilities.

We will discuss this in more detail in a later chapter. Here we need to underscore that Satan, the god of this world, has blinded minds, not only to the glorious gospel of Christ (2 Cor. 4:4), but also to God's glory in the church (Eph. 3:21). Cleverly, Satan has lulled vast segments of the church into such a stupor that decline, attrition, and forgetfulness seem normal. The adversary has taken away any dynamic view of the community of the kingdom of God and replaced it with a comfortable notion of this familiar place and these familiar people who maintain religion for its own sake.

The kingdom pastor, the pastor-evangelist, enters the scene as visionary and as sculptor in Word and prayer. The kingdom pastor has the evangelizing task, in Ellul's words,[6] of "subverting the subversion." This means deliberately and patiently forming in the corporate mind of the congregation a biblical image of the church, the vision given on the mount. The kingdom pastor highlights the tragedy of the subtle satanic work that reduces Christ's church to less than a community of alternative and missionary and kingdom consciousness.

We need to remind ourselves again of how marvelously self-aware Jesus was: he knew who he was, where he had come from, what he had to do, where his mandate came from, what the future held (see John 6). This same calling and awareness belongs to the church. But that is the furtherest thing from the minds of most congregations.

I Will Build My Church

If we look for the pattern given on the mount in the New Testament documents, we become aware of how much *eisegesis*[7] has taken place—reading into rather than out of the text. The church over the centuries has often read its own self-understanding into Scripture.[8] When we look at the New Testament documents *exegetically*[9] and read out of the text rather than into it, we find that the church was *assumed* but hardly ever described in any way to satisfy our scholastic desires. The church we glimpse in the New Testament was diverse, imperfect, struggling, and awesome. But it was always in process. As F. R. Maltby so colorfully put it, the New Testament church was "absurdly happy, completely fearless, and constantly in trouble."[10]

However, the church is never formally defined. The form and order appear flexible and differ from place to place. We see primarily a *missionary* church, seldom more than one generation removed from its apostolic and missionary beginnings. This church was deeply bound to its Hebrew heritage, even when it moved into new areas. When surrounded by a Greek or pagan culture, it was regularly in prophetic confrontation with that culture.

Our churches in North America (and Europe) are many generations from their origins and increasingly oblivious to the biblical narrative. They have traditions and denominational or ideological wineskins that don't easily accommodate creativity in changing cultures or neighborhoods. Such congregations have long forgotten any missionary calling or awareness of their missionary context. They are often more like denominational franchises.

It is obvious in the New Testament documents that congregations had pastor-teachers but no church buildings, no huge endowment funds, and no clergy establishment, in a formal sense. They lacked external props! If a church was alive, it was alive. If it died, it literally passed out of existence. If it was alive (not perfect, just alive), you knew it. If it was dead, it was difficult to fool anybody.

Jesus never prescribed forms for the church. He did assume his disciples would live in community under his word. The Hebrew focus on the community over the individual was a presupposition. Still, we must tease out what Jesus might have wanted such a community to look like. He did make clear the church's *calling, purpose, and mission.* At Caesarea Philippi, after Peter's affirmation that Jesus *was* the long-awaited Messiah, Jesus responded with the cryptic statement that on that rock he would build his church.

The ordinary Greek word *ekklēsia* pertains to any assembly called for a purpose, such as a town meeting or, in the Greek version of the Old Testament, the congregation of Israel. An assembly or community of faith is a significant part of Christ's mission, of the *pattern.* The "I will build" part of the statement, however, resounds with sovereign good purpose. The sovereign Lord will create such a community, notwithstanding the foibles, infidelities, and weaknesses of its human members.

That gives us hope! That's *ecclesiology,* the calling of God's new community. The sovereign Lord calls. It is his work. It is a call out of one dominion into another; a call to repentance and to a radical newness. At the other end of Jesus' teachings and of the pattern is *missiology,* the sending of the new community. "As the Father has sent me, I am sending you" (John 20:21). "All authority . . . has been given unto me. . . . Therefore go and make disciples of all nations. . . . And surely I am with you always" (Matt. 28:18-20). The kingdom pastor will see in God's pattern on the mount the linkage between being *called out* and being *sent out,* between ecclesiology and missiology.

First-generation Christians and Christian communities are more likely (though not guaranteed) to remember their calling out of paganism (Eph. 2:2) into Christ's dominion. This vocation is both individual and communal. The sovereign Lord commands repentance, faith, and an alternative way of thinking and living. We are to "turn from the power of Satan to God" (Acts 26:18). Jesus has "a totalitarian claim" on our lives. Paul can even count us as Christ's slaves (1 Cor. 7:22) and call pastors to be "slaves" of their people "for Jesus' sake" (2 Cor. 4:5, NRSV).

The renunciation of evil in many baptismal traditions is a reminder of Christ's claim upon believers: "Do you renounce Satan and the forces of wickedness that rebel against God? Do you renounce the evil powers of this world which corrupt and destroy God's creatures?"[11]

The calling is also *into* the dynamically present reign of God. The called-out people of God are the community of the kingdom of God. As such, they need to be formed and informed by the *missiological* dimension of that calling. "As the Father has sent me, I am sending you" (John 20:21).

The disciples and the apostles were the church in its infancy. Jesus breathed on them and said, "Receive the

Holy Spirit." The church is to be the Word of God made visible, grace and truth incarnate, a people of the cross, self-sacrificing love, as Jesus was. The apostle extols the power of the Spirit at work in the church and exclaims, "To him be glory in the church and in Christ Jesus" (Eph. 3:21). God is to be glorified in his church as God is in his Son. "As the Father has sent me, I am sending you."

• • •

Friend Ben was pensive. "I'm listening. When I look at my wonderful congregation through the grid of what makes a 'successful church,' I've got one. My members are socially a neat bunch. They engage in a lot of good stuff. Institutionally, we lead the pack in our presbytery. I'm applauded by everybody for the effective job I've done. Yet in the light of what we're looking at here, the church is so far from the Vision."

"Don't overdo the worry, Ben," I assured him. "You're beginning to see what kingdom pastors are all about. All congregations are to some degree in the same plight. They are a mixture. The mind-set of church people keeps reverting to categories of power, success, and security that are alien to Christ's kingdom. Even Christ's disciples struggled to understand him. Sometimes Jesus asked, 'Do you still not understand?' That is how and why kingdom pastors are always evangelists, calling the church to what it is intended to be.

"The task is never completed. But once you see it, Ben, you know the Vision is pulling you in the right direction. When you're aware of the dominion of evil, you won't be oppressed by a conspiracy theory. Instead, you can walk through it with thanksgiving and praise, mirth, and joy, because Jesus is Lord. You know that "now the prince of this world will be driven out" (John 12:31). The

Lamb of God who suffers is the Lion of Judah; he shall reign forever (Rev. 5). Meanwhile, our mission is to be faithful in calling the people of God to the Vision."

Pattern: The John 17 Prayer

The twin concepts of *ecclesiology* and *missiology* are only the broad parameters of our quest. The insistent and persistent question is what the church, this community of the kingdom of God, looks like. How is it visibly the glory of God? What is the pattern given on the mount? Where do we find that pattern?

Lesslie Newbigin has a marvelous description of the congregation as the hermeneutic of the gospel, the group that interprets the good news. He spells out visible characteristics of such a congregation.[12] But the mount indicates that something graphic in Scriptures gives the pattern. Perhaps it is found in Christ's high priestly prayer (John 17). This prayer includes what Christ wills for his people. In the incarnation or expression of these petitions, we find evidences of Christ's life in his people. I see five characteristics that are to be incarnate in God's people and are part of the pattern.

1. Amid the hurt and brokenness of humanity, the church is to be a people of *joy*—not just a so-so joy, but "the full measure of my joy within them" (John 17:13). In *Naught for Your Comfort,* Huddleston told how his Cape Town congregation of blacks, though oppressed under apartheid, was dancing in the streets for joy. The church is set free from the power of darkness and transferred into the kingdom of the beloved Son of God (Col. 1:13). Believers have ecstatic and profound joy, even in the most unlikely settings.

2. The people of God are formed, informed, and transformed (sanctified) by the *truth* (17:17) of God's word as spoken by, incarnated in, and interpreted through Jesus Christ. Contemporary theologians such as George Lindbeck, Hans Frei, Stanley Hauerwas, and others are reminding us that the people of God are formed out of the biblical narrative. This also becomes their message (17:20). The biblical story of Israel, Jesus, and the apostles becomes the church's story; it forms the church's life and faith and identity. The word of God, the truth of God, is to become incarnate in the church in every new generation.

3. "I have given them the glory that you gave me" (17:22). I believe the Holy Spirit is the *glory* Jesus has given his church. This passage has been much discussed and is enigmatic. But the apostle Peter later refers to the "Spirit of glory and of God" (1 Peter 4:14). There are many scriptural teachings about the Holy Spirit as the one who creates the church in the image of God. I believe Jesus envisioned a church energized to be God's new creation, just as he was energized by the Father. The church is supernaturally endowed to be the light shining in the darkness.[13]

4. "May they be brought to complete unity" (17:23). The working out of this *unity* is intimidating, given the fragmentation of the one holy catholic and apostolic church and the dissension within traditions and particular congregations. But unity is also a major witness to the world. This relational witness of the church to the world emerges previously in John 13:34-35. It is painfully obvious that we sin in falling short of our Lord's desire for the unity of his own people. If, as some suggest, all these petitions are to be answered before our Lord returns, then a lot of walls must come down.

5. Finally, Jesus wants costly, unconditional, forgiving, and self-sacrificing *love.* "Righteous Father, though the world does not know you, I know you, and they know that you have sent me. I have made you known to them, and will continue to make you known *in order that the love you* *have for me may be in them, and that I myself may be in them"* (17:25-26, emphasis added). This petition is set in the context of those outside: "the world (*kosmos*) does not know you," the Father. Jesus tells the Father about his own evangelizing ministry to make believers become vessels of divine love. Such love is to be the character of the people of God. They are loved by the Father as the Son is loved, and they are to be the "dwelling place of God" (cf. Eph. 2:22).

The purpose of the Savior of sinners is to create a community marked by joy, truth, glory, unity, divine love, and divine residence. For humans, this seems impossible. The kingdom pastor needs to see the pattern, to look beyond *what is* to *what shall be*. The kingdom pastor needs to realize that Satan will target the church's strong points!

Pattern: Faith, Love, Hope

A similar set of grids is often found in the epistles and provides a description of the character of the people of God: *faith, hope, and love.*[14] Each word is a mine to explore.

• ***Faith*** is the church's commitment to truth as set forth in Holy Scriptures and in Jesus Christ. The church is committed to a message, the revelation of God in Christ, the story of Israel and of Jesus the Messiah, the apostolic preaching (*kerygma*). The people of God are not free to believe whatever they want. I recently heard a person boast that she likes her church because you are free to believe whatever you want to believe. Alas!

Today there is an inclination toward antirealism, meaning that God and faith are what I want them to be. I construct them in my image; there is no objective reality or revelation that makes them what they are. I reinterpret Scripture to make it mean what I choose and to fit my own values and prejudices.

God's people worship with their minds and offer

their minds in the service of God. They are intellectually curious, imaginative, and exploratory. But their faith and their commitment to truth is like an inertial guidance system that enables them to know where *home* is. Faith grows dim when the corporate church doesn't know God's revelation in Christ and in Scripture, when spiritual and theological formations are replaced with popular, market-driven church programs.

• ***Hope*** is the church's commitment to God's purpose, design, and kingdom. It is the certainty based on the church being *God's mission.* Hope and faith feed each other (cf. Heb. 11:1). Hope is commitment to the fact that "God is working his purpose out as year succeeds to year."[15] Hope is a commitment in mission, looking to the day when "the earth shall be full of the knowledge of the Lord as the waters cover the sea" (Isa. 11:9).

Hope is the church dynamic. Hope burst forth at the resurrection of Christ and affirmed that God has triumphed over the powers of this world, so we are no longer locked in darkness. Hope continually breaks the chains of the inevitable, the chains of bondage to yesterday and today. Hope sets the people of God free to see beyond the Valley of Achor to the Door of Hope. Hope is the church seeing itself and the world with missiological eyes.

• • •

"Time out! Hold it. Wow! Let me digest some of this," Debbie broke in. "First of all, I'm hearing a signal that is rebuking me more than a little. The word *truth* in the John 17 passage, the word *faith,* and now your definition of *hope*—these are beginning to convict me. They point out how lightly I have dealt with my need. I need knowledge and skill to communicate Scripture effectively. I also need ways to help my congregation clarify our call to mission."

Andy and Ben said that such priorities had become buried in all the *shoulds* and *oughts* of their work.

Debbie went on, "I think I hear a suggestion that we need continually to stand back from the present expression of congregational life. We need to look through eyes of *hope*. This raises questions: What does Christ want to accomplish in this Christian community? Am I convinced it shall be so? In accord with John 15, do I have that I-in-Christ, Christ's-word-in-me, Christ-in-me kind of intimacy, so I am convinced that the fruit of God will come forth? Have I been shabby on that one? I'm not sure seminary did much to focus me on it."

Ben asked, "Am I reading you correctly? Are you suggesting that a significant and subtle part of the spiritual conflict is in this quiet erosion of truth and hope, so the church can exist 'successfully' without relation to God's truth or mission? Is that where you're going?"

"Hang in there, guys. We'll get to that. Let's deal with love first."

• • •

• ***Love*** is the great commandment and the church's commitment to real people: sinful, lost, confused, despairing, vain, posturing, proud, rebellious human beings. "God so loved . . . that whoever. . . ." (John 3:16). Jesus came not to call the righteous but sinners to repentance and into the Father's family (Mark 2:17). Charles Schultz's moppet Lucy protests, "I love humanity; it's people I can't stand!" The church is committed to the *nobodies*, the exasperating individuals who don't know who they are or what they want.

The Bible tells of a God who is plenteous in love and mercy, then ends on this note: "The Spirit and the bride say, 'Come!' And let him who hears say, 'Come!' Whoever is thirsty, let him come, and whoever wishes, let him take of the free gift of the water of life" (Rev. 22:17). The church as a community of love incarnates the new creation.

Faith, hope, and love. Truth, God's tomorrow, and real persons. These are essential commitments. Leave any out, and a wasting sickness sets in. If we focus only on one commitment and diminish the others, we block out some light and let some darkness intrude into the church. When all are present and self-consciously nurtured, we build according to the pattern given on the mount.

• • •

"Before we go on, Bob," Andy broke in, "I'm resonating with your theory. I buy it. But face it, membership as we have it today (at least in my church) has little to do with the disciplines you're showing us from Scripture. In most churches I know, any community disciplines or formations are puny. Accountability and responsibility are virtually unknown. Membership means little more than privilege and access to the rites and ministries of the congregation. Even in large congregations such as Ben's, I bet the congregational privilege of voting is an empty formality. And feathers are ruffled if demands are made. Am I right?"

"You're right. A practical part of the discipline we're seeking as kingdom pastors is how to hold each other accountable for fidelity to the John 17 pattern or the faith-hope-love pattern. This could force us back to an earlier, unsettling question: Have we trivialized membership until neither repentance nor faith are expected?"[16]

• • •

Pattern: The Marks of the Church

Thus far we have looked at the Bible for the pattern. In recent decades, as the church has examined its history, Scriptures, the church's essence, and God's pattern for its life and faithfulness, there has emerged an understanding of the *marks* or *signs* of the church. There are variations on this understanding, depending on whom you read.[17] These marks are succinct and well-balanced descriptions of the pattern of the church. They provide a ready set of criteria for evaluating the faithfulness of a given church in its ecclesiology-missiology.

The marks are *kerygma, leitourgia, diakonia, marturia,* and *koinonia*—apostolic message, worship, ministry of human compassion, witness, and community that is interdependent and accountable. These are similar to the biblical grids we have already discussed (see Acts 2—7).

• ***Kerygma*** or preaching refers to the basic apostolic message which forms, informs, and transforms the church's corporate and individual life. It is always centered in the cross of Jesus Christ and contains the data, demands, and promises of the apostolic preaching of Christ.

Jesus preached, taught, and served the inbreaking kingdom of God and moved inexorably to his cross. In his resurrection, he triumphed over principalities and powers, the death of death. He atoned for our sins and the sins of the world. He brought reconciliation between God and humankind and put into effect the New Covenant.

The epistles called this the preaching of Christ, of Christ crucified, who brings *salvation* and resurrection life. The church is called into being and given its reason for being by this preaching and teaching of Christ. It is here that the church establishes its apostolicity.

• ***Leitourgia*** is worship. The church is the church as it offers itself to God in worship. The church's life flows out of this ministry to God. The New Testament begins with Mary, then the shepherds, responding to God in worship. It ends with the myriads in heaven giving praise to God and to the Lamb. In the human pilgrimage, the church responds to God's salvation in worship, songs, prayers, Scriptures, and the Lord's Supper—"lost in wonder, love, and praise."

• ***Diakonia*** is the expression of God's compassion toward human tragedy and need. "Whatever you did for one of the least of these brothers of mine" (Matt. 25:40) sets apart those who follow Christ from those who do not. Jesus' ministry to the helpless, crushed, hungry, blind, leprous, dead, and poor (Luke 7:21-23) becomes the church's ministry. It is a significant part of the John 20:21 commission. Diakonia is demonstrated in the Acts accounts and prophetically preached to the church by the apostle James.

• ***Marturia*** is witness, a mission outward. New Testament documents clearly are written to the community of faith, to call it to faithfulness and holiness. Subtly they call the church to live before the watching world, before men and women, so that they may "see your good deeds and praise your Father in heaven" (Matt. 5:16). "You will be my witnesses in Jerusalem, and in all Judea and Samaria, and to the ends of the earth" (Acts 1:8). "Live such good lives among the pagans that, though they accuse you of doing wrong, they may see your good deeds and glorify God on the day he visits us" (1 Pet. 2:12). God desires that his glory be reflected through the lives of his people. This shines forth in Scriptures as early as the calling of Abraham (Gen. 12:1-3).

William Temple said that the church exists for those outside of itself. D. T. Niles spoke of the church as existing for witness as a fire for burning. But notice how quickly this becomes a non-concern in congregations and even denominations. Why? What is the source of such resistance and blindness to the mandate to *marturia*?

• ***Koinonia*** refers to the unique, interdependent community in which Christians share their lives in self-giving and costly love. The word *fellowship* so often used to translate koinonia has become banal. It more often refers to a coffee hour or a church supper. Koinonia has depth and dimension. The church in its relational dimension is the body of Christ, where all things are held in common, and where if one member suffers, all suffer. Koinonia refers to redeemed society, where privatism is eschewed, where we bear each other's burdens, where we live out the command to love each other as Christ loves us. This is the communal mark and sign of the church.

• • •

I told my three colleagues that the tendency to downgrade these marks is a significant factor in the conflict with the powers of darkness and in the integrity of their pastoral ministry. Many church members have little awareness of these marks. John 17, faith-hope-love, and the marks of the church—all these patterns presuppose God. They assume a dynamic and living God, involved with his new humanity, his *ekklēsia,* his church. This God provides ongoing deliverance out of the dominion of Satan and into the dominion of God.

"I'm trying to process all of this with who I am and with the congregation God has called me to serve," Andy said. "But it's like an overlay. I lay these patterns of ecclesiology and missiology on top of the actual congregation, and it's like two worlds. One is God's world.

"The other is my congregation that exists so much as part of the worldly social fabric. There is the security structure of the lives of the members, the families, the nation, economics, and all the idols of our culture. In that world, God is missing. The church exists to exist! I'm not accusing my people. If I'm honest, I don't expect any demonstration of God's Spirit and power (1 Cor. 2:4). That's an alien idea to me and to the church. It's all strictly human: 'This is how we do it in business, and so this is how it should be done in the church.' "

"The expectations I sense from denominational agencies aren't much improvement," Debbie noted. "Even worship means having the proper form of the rites. Fads and trendy stuff from the cultural ethos get passed along in 'exciting' new programs and conferences. But often they don't seem to come from the Bible. I don't want to downgrade my denomination, but the mission of God doesn't seem to determine what we're supposed to be doing."

"Yeah," Ben chimed in. "So I'm a successful manager, an effective CEO of a neat institution. God bless us all! But it doesn't connect with what we've been talking about."

"Now you are getting the picture," I said. "This isn't some new pattern of conflict. You'll find it in Paul's teaching about the Spirit and the flesh. At the heart of these two worlds, as Andy put it, is the tendency to reduce the 'dwelling place in which God lives by his Spirit' (Eph. 2:22) to a merely human institution, then to make it comfortable in its worldly habitat.

"The irony here is that the church as called can *never* be comfortable with or acceptable to the dominant structures of its habitat. Righteous living is a judgment upon unrighteousness. For defensive reasons, the darkness of the world continues to resent or hate Christians who live out their calling to be a new creation.[18] When the church makes peace with its setting and becomes comfortable, it abandons its calling by God. The church becomes a religion without God, without being called and transferred from one dominion to another (Col. 1:13).

"But make no mistake. Here where we live, in the

overlap of the ages, the church is always in the presence of both dominions. Do you begin to see why our calling is to be *pastor-evangelists*? Congregations such as yours are continually in this conflict. They need to be reminded of the calling of God, of the nature of God's mission, of their purpose in the plan of God. This task never ends. Congregations need to be thrilled again and again with what God in Christ has done, is doing, and will yet do. In this joyous awareness, the church is really free. But there's one more pattern."

Pattern: Sermon on the Mount

Roman Catholic pastor-theologian Segundo Galilea makes a beautiful case for the church's life and witness being formed by the Sermon on the Mount, especially the Beatitudes.[19] I like it! A kingdom-shaped community ought to be the demonstration of that sermon; the implications are almost too radical and awesome to envision.

Maybe the church in North America can be shrugged off so easily because that church tends to treat the Sermon-on-the-Mount pattern as unlivable. We are immersed in a society abounding with idols: middle-class values, the American way of life, market capitalism, American interests abroad, the consumer society, self-fulfillment, and others. Meanwhile, our Lord's primary sermon (Matt. 5-7; Luke 6:17-49) describes kingdom people as identifying with the poor. He points to the perils of being rich, and expects zeal for justice, mercy, and peacemaking—seeking *first* God's kingdom and righteousness.

This remarkable sermon speaks of a profound affinity for the moral law of God. It gives guidance in such specific areas as the sanctity of life and marriage (Matt. 5:27-32) and loving enemies (5:44). It sets a norm for generosity to the needy as well as a life of fasting and prayer (6:1-17). Most shocking, Jesus names money (mammon), one of our favorite idols, as a primary competitor to the worship of God (6:24). In addition, Jesus says that orthodox theology or miraculous accomplishments aren't enough (7:22). Rather, out of identification with Christ himself, true disciples express a primary zeal for the reign of God and his justice, for true Sermon-on-the-Mount living. Then all things shall be theirs (6:33).

The pattern for the church in the Sermon on the Mount is more complex than the graphic and easily remembered categories discussed earlier. But if we are to be followers of Jesus, it can't be dismissed—though much of the church has tried to do just that. The Sermon on the Mount is offensive to the common mind-set and lifestyles of this age. Too often in our pastoral zeal not to offend, we quietly mute one or more kingdom principles. In so doing, we allow the agenda of *this age* to prevail. Then the Spirit is quenched, the light is hidden.

However, a kingdom-shaped community is called to be a demonstration of Jesus' Sermon on the Mount.

Conclusion

I described the two catalytic events influencing my pilgrimage: the corporate principle and the exhortation to "build according to the pattern given on the mount." The kingdom pastor looks at his Valley of Achor congregation through these eyes. She sees it by faith. The kingdom pastor is like a Michelangelo looking at a large chunk of marble and seeing in it a Pieta or a David. He has the pattern in mind before sculpting the dream, the Vision. It is a long-term effort in Word, prayer, and patience, chipping away, remembering that "weeping may remain for a night, but rejoicing comes in the morning" (Ps. 30:5b).

The kingdom pastor is like Israel on the plains of Moab before the conquest of Canaan, with Moses giving them the Second Law and reminding them that the conquest will come through faithful obedience. Still we hear, "The Lord will drive out those nations before you, little by little. You will not be allowed to eliminate them all at once, or the wild animals will multiply around you" (Deut. 7:22).

The kingdom pastor is like me in my impatience and zeal as an organic gardener. I look at the unlikely patch of yellow clay in my yard and visualize what will be reality. Ten years of disciplines will produce dark fertile soil and nourish lovely plants that flourish and bloom.

The *pattern given* is the set of spectacles the kingdom pastor wears to see the task assigned. Because the context is not neutral, we often meet devastating discouragement. The dominion of Satan is not passive. There are subtle and not-so-subtle pathologies which challenge, discourage, and destroy.

• • •

But that's for next time. "Oh, yes! For heaven's sake, time out!" Andy blurted. "I have a bad case of sensory overload. Let's call it quits for tonight."

So with laughter and prayer together, we did exactly that.

6

Pathologies in the Church

"WE NEED to ask some basic questions at the outset," I began on our next evening together. "How does this conflict appear in the church? How is it explained?

"Andy, the clue is in your quote from Franz Overbeck. If the church is the embodiment of Christ and the gospel, what was it that so rankled the powers that they executed Jesus? Why would they destroy one who went about doing good? They either didn't understand what was going on (2 Cor. 2:7-8), or they understood well enough to know that they were losing their own power (Acts 4:24-31; Col. 2:15).

"We must deal with all those warnings to his disciples about the hate that would be directed at them because Jesus came as Word and Light (John 15:18-25). We have adopted a model of church that doesn't confront the evil in a social-political-cultural-economic scene. It is co-opted by this present age, blessing every war that comes along. This world loves a culture of darkness and resents and even hates anyone or any community that doesn't play by its rules. And the church tries to be cozy with such a world!

"Overbeck put his finger on this in saying that 'all Christian theology . . . is unchristian and satanic, since it draws Christianity into the sphere of civilization and culture.' "

"All well and good," Ben said, "but get real! For all these centuries, at least since the fourth century, we've thought of the church as the wholesome companion of state and culture. You're suggesting the church has been deceived all this time? Hey, you could be proposing a new cult that has rediscovered the true church. What do we do with my congregation, which is comfortable with North American culture and values?"

"What about Overbeck,[1] Kierkegaard,[2] Hauerwas, Willimon,[3] and the radical Anabaptists disagreeing with the sixteenth-century Reformers, who let church and culture be married?" wondered Debby. "Perhaps they were far more correct than we imagined. Is it possible that nearly everything we're doing in the church is alien to the true intent of Christ? That's almost too much to accept."

"I need to know," stressed Andy, "whether I can arrive at some kingdom integrity and still function as the pastor of a church that piously resists the alternative demands of the kingdom of God. Can anybody? If I try, what happens? How does the antipathy between dominions show up?"

"Okay, let's take a stab at it," I responded.

• • •

In J. R. R. Tolkein's delightful epic *The Lord of the Rings*, there are colorful creatures, somewhere between humans and trees, called *ents*. They're more botanical than zoological, but they talk and walk. They're robust and wise and long-lived. They play a strategic role at a critical juncture in the story. The ents are passing out of existence. They lament that forces at work are "making mere trees out of ents!"

Is it possible that nearly everything we're doing in the church is "making mere trees out of ents"? Are we creating mere religious enclaves out of churches that should be a "dwelling in which God lives by his Spirit" (Eph. 2:22), the community and embodiment of the reign of God in present history and culture? And our continual controversies in the church—are they over the wrong concerns?

In our congregations are two realities, the wine and the wineskin. The wineskin can exist without the wine of the gospel. But the wine cannot exist without the wineskin, without some form, some community in which it is contained, embodied, and practiced.

One of these realities is the visible, controllable, organizable form. It has institutional life. It is "merely human"[4] or humanly explainable. It grows by marketing. A pastor is a custodian, manager, and public relations professional. This form can exist and prosper without reference to the gospel that is supposed to be its reason for being.

The other reality is the wine of the gospel and the dynamic dwelling place of the Spirit. It is people who have heard the promises and demands of the gospel and are being transformed by it. This reality cannot exist without a wineskin, without form. This congregation in Christ is seen only by the eyes of faith; it is discernible only by the Spirit, by faith. It is humanly uncontrollable because it is the communion in the Holy Spirit (John 3:8; 2 Cor. 3:17). God keeps breaking in and breaking out, upsetting schedules and organization.

This makes true church an adventure of faith into the unknown and into hope. In such a reality, God makes disciples, calls forth obedience, and creates his instruments of the gospel in ways that are not always expected or visible (1 Cor. 12:11). In this community the "powers of the coming age" (Heb. 6:5) are at work.

Such an assembly has true kingdom consciousness. This community is not captive to the dominant social order, not conformed to the spirits of this age. In this reality, the pastor is an intercessor who uses word and prayer to make a community of faith, hope, and love. The pastor walks by faith and is controlled by the Spirit. The church grows through the preaching of Christ, true evangelism, and the spontaneity of the gospel. This reality becomes larger when the Spirit dominates.

Yet wine and wineskin remain one, existing as visible form and invisible interior. The problem is that what is *seen* tends pathologically to overwhelm the *unseen*. Every congregation is a combination of the two. Where the unseen is dominant, we are becoming like the Door of Hope Church; where the seen dominates, we are like the Valley of Achor. The seen is good only as formed by the unseen. The wine of the gospel is alive and transforming, and it requires new wineskins, adaptable ones.

Alas, the old wineskin takes on a life of its own. The institution eclipses the gospel it exists to enhance. Many classic creeds and liturgies of the church say little about the church's *vocation* and its *mission*. They say little about missiology and ecclesiology, about how this institution relates to what God in Christ purposes to accomplish with humankind. What the creeds say is true, but what they fail to say reveals a blindness about God's intention for his people.

Check the Te Deum, the Apostles' and Nicene creeds, the Westminster Confession of Faith. Even the liturgies of the eucharist can mute the church's apostolate. The pattern is custodial. The dynamic and apostolic conception of the church as *sent* is muted in the church's pilgrimage. Thus the Valley of Achor churches resist costly obedience beyond their own walls.

Often congregations drive to church buildings that are islands in "white harvest fields," densely populated and often blighted urban areas. They ignore the mission at their doorstep and try to maintain familiar places with familiar faces. The idea that the church, like Christ, is called out (*ek-klēsia*) to be sent (John 20:21), that it has an apostolate,[5] upsets the church as Paul upset the mob at Thessalonica. "These people who have been turning the world upside down have come here also" (Acts 17:6, NRSV). Likewise, Ahab said to Elijah, "Is that you, you troubler of Israel?" (1 Kings 18:17).

It is all right if others want to come into our congregations if they come in quietly, bolster our numbers and income, and adopt our lifestyle, our traditions, and our ethos. If they change us or make demands on us—alas! Hans Küng notes that the church resists and expunges enthusiasts and renewalists.[6] The same is true also of proponents of transformation, reformation, growth, and kingdom obedience.[7] It is especially true in Valley of Achor churches.

This subject relates to our sojourn into joy! I am not wallowing in pathologies as an exercise in ecclesiastical and pastoral masochism. But especially in North America, the church, though apparently large and vigorous, is dysfunctional and declining[8] as a culture-transforming community of the kingdom of God. The kingdom pastor needs to be wide awake to ever-present sickness.

• • •

We four dreamers (Acts 2:17) stopped to process where we had been. We lamented that the message of Christ, the mission of God, and the heart of God were hardly determining factors in the lives of our congregation. That almost sounds like an overstatement. But when we explored what motivated our congregations in their corporate lives, it seldom started with searching Scripture for these factors.

"Institutional prosperity is seductive, isn't it?" asked Ben. "My church members like my preaching when it's clever and quotable and they can brag about it to their friends. But they seldom encourage me to spend time with them in transformational disciplines and Bible study. The same is true of the decisions we make about congregational life. And mind you, we have about as complete a congregational life as one church can produce. People are joining, and we have programs for everyone."

"I think that's par for the course," Debbie commented. "One church in our presbytery does something novel that attracts attention. Soon, whether or not it has a shred of connection with the mission of Christ, it's cloned in church after church until it runs its course. Then the next fad comes along. I sometimes feel like a promotion agency."

"It's a bit different in my congregation," Andy observed. "My people are preservers of cultural traditions. They fear change. Some of that's good, but certain traditions are a real drag, and no one remembers when or why they were started—just that 'we've always done it that way.' However, the familiarity of it is almost sacred. This is particularly true in music—a sacrosanct province in most churches. Some music is meaningless to a new generation and doctrinally questionable to begin with. Boy-o-boy, can I stir up a hornet's nest by tampering with that one. But that's the point we're making, isn't it? There is subtle pressure to do things that are *not bad* but that nevertheless run counter the mission of God. Right?"

"Yes, you've identified part of the tension we're dealing with," I noted. "Kingdom pastors need to preserve traditions that carry the new *wine*, and discover and prune off those that use up energy without purpose. Why are congregations so resistant to discerning what expresses the disobedient side of culture? Why do so many church activities have no relation to the gospel?"

• • •

Deliver Us from the Evil One

We claim to take the Bible seriously as the church's primary source of the apostolic faith. Then, however we describe Scripture—whether as the Word of God written, the infallible rule of faith and practice, the witness to the revelation of God—we cannot with integrity avoid biblical teaching about the devil. "The reason the Son of God appeared was to destroy the devil's work" (1 John 3:8b).

I can accept the questions and the mystery surrounding this teaching of the devil, enigmatic and perplexing as it is. Others have done extensive exegetical work on this fascinating subject.[9] In kingdom ministry, Jesus and the apostles recognized the opposition of a supernatural and destructive personality. The devil or Satan is *the god of this world* (2 Cor. 4:4) and the enemy of the church (1 Pet. 5:8). But he and his underlings are doomed through God's triumph in Christ.[10] At the same time, God can make the devil serve his sovereign purpose in redemption, as mysterious as that seems (cf. Job 1–2; John 13:27; Rom. 11:11).

The kingdom pastor cannot interpret one's task or the church apart from awareness of conflict with "the god of this age" (2 Cor. 4:4). The Lord's Prayer petitions the Father to "deliver us from the evil one" (Matt. 6:13). The devil is a destructive presence, one who erodes, accuses, discourages, blinds, subverts, lies, murders, counterfeits, destroys, and inhabits death. This evil one persistently obscures the message, calling, and mission of the church.

New Testament Scriptures are replete with references to this evil power. What negative force is at work? Why do churches tend to become more indifferent with the passing generations, rather than stronger? What eroding effect "makes mere trees out of ents"? Why the symptoms of destruction? Baptismal formulas still contain the renunciation of "Satan and all the spiritual forces of wickedness that rebel against God, and the evil powers of this world, which corrupt and destroy the creatures of God." Is that a throwback to a less sophisticated time?

What malignant force energizes evil? What is the nature of "the kingdom of the air" (Eph. 2:2)? I do not have glib answers. Probe the reality of such biblical themes as darkness, death, and mystery. Look at Paul's lament over Israel (Rom. 9) as he reminds his readers that the Israelites were adopted as God's children. The divine glory (*shekinah*), the covenants, the law, the temple worship, the promises, and the patriarchs belonged to them. The human ancestry of Jesus is traced through them.

So awesome are these gifts that Paul interrupts his discourse to glorify the one "who is God over all, forever praised! Amen" (9:5). Then he goes on, "It is not as though God's word had failed. For not all who are descended from Israel are Israel." From there he plunges into the mystery of faith, election, disobedience, and spiritual blindness.

The point I wish to make here has to do with the *mystery* (Rom. 11:25) of subtle erosion from the reality of covenant faith, reducing it to merely outward form, then to disobedience. Finally comes divine sternness (11:22). In Romans 9–11, Israel is still in God's covenantal purpose, yet set aside for a time, in hope that later Israel will believe. Those who receive God's mercy must never take that for granted. The Door of Hope Church is always one generation away from being the Valley of Achor Church.

Can the reality of saving faith live for more than one generation? Is there a *dis-evangelizing* force at work in this age of death that continually tries to destroy faith? The church resists even asking the question! The church resists reformers or co-opts and tames them. Even parachurch movements or independent church expressions of a fresher faith soon become like the rest.

William Stringfellow has suggested that churches can become principalities and powers when they demand for themselves a devotion that belongs only to God.[11] Good things can become idols, distractions, and competitors for worship and devotion to God. Examples are clergy, buildings, theology, theologians, church institutions, liturgies, sacraments, seminary training and degrees, even revivals and awakenings. They become self-perpetuating distractions that keep the church from being the glory of God. Often they have little to do with God's salvation.

Deliver us from the evil one!

What part do Satan and the evil powers play in this diminishing process in every congregation? What false and subliminal assumptions are of death and seduce the church? How can we diagnose the pathologies of unbelief? of personal and interpersonal sin within the church? of corporate disobedience such as racism? of cultural idols such as nation, economy, and way of life? Suppose you become pastor of a Valley of Achor church. It looks all right. The ecclesiastical furniture is in place, but that critical intangible is absent. All of the patterns are merely human. Why?

Church history shows how quickly the church forsook grace, reduced the divine-human mystery of Jesus, adopted clericalism, slid into superstitions, distorted God's sovereignty, accepted reductionist views of the seriousness of human depravity, and often became captive of a bourgeois, wealthy culture. In our own time, we have become indifferent to the church's calling to loving relationships and to true righteousness and justice. In our relationship to God, we have avoided holiness and forsaken true worship. We put no emphasis on the new self, renewed in knowledge in the image of the Creator (Col. 3:10).

The source of the trouble is Satan, working through our selfish desires to bring death (James 1:13-15). The dominion of Satan is real. The gates of death and hell do attempt to prevail against the church. Malignancy surrounds our life together as the people of God. Fallenness pervades the culture. There is no Christian nation, only nations in which for brief moments the church, as the salt and light, prevails. Then spiritual darkness intrudes into the church, and the light within becomes dark (Matt. 6:22-23).

When the darkness comes inside the church, it becomes even more hazardous for the pastor to seek to exalt the light! The battle between the Lamb and the Beast persists (Rev. 13). Only by faith do we know that the triumph belongs to the Lamb. But in the process, the saints of God and the kingdom pastors in every generation cry out, "How long, O Lord?" (Rev. 6:10).

Our Struggle Is Not Against Flesh and Blood

Spiritual conflict is viewed from many perspectives. In the conservative Protestantism of my youth, it was viewed it as an explanation for personal and interpersonal difficulties and for irrational personalities. It lacked something in practical reality. Yet we realized the biblical principle that something destructive was going on. We acknowledged spiritual conflict even when we didn't understand it.

I have read of the witnessing church in the Republic of South Africa, of Tutu and Boesak and those (before recent accords to dismantle apartheid) who accepted the lordship of Christ. The most obvious principalities and powers were the external forces of government and policies of apartheid. The late William Stringfellow and his disciples made a valid point that destructive institutions and social-cultural forces that require allegiance are principalities and powers.

Liberation theologians make a good case that the Ephesian letter is written in the context of the Roman government and the pressures of that government upon the infant church. This is corroborated by the Johannine teaching in Revelation that the "beast out of the sea" represents anti-Christian governments that seek to seduce or destroy the church (Rev. 13).

Church consultants often lead us to think that if we can resolve church conflicts through conflict resolution, we are home free. They assume that fruitful ministry is hindered by a clash between pastor and board, or between pastor and congregation. That may be true. It may also be the beginning place for the kingdom pastor. If the pastor has diseased relationships with the congregation and congregational leadership, there is a poor foundation for any other redemptive work. However, the flaw here is the assumption that the context of these relationships is neutral and is congenial to the light.

The principalities and powers mentioned in Ephesians 6 seem to be far more than the obviously destructive, demeaning, and deceptive forces in the valid but limited interpretations explored above. Imagine that the Valley of Achor Church is loving, well-organized, and completely happy—but spiritually blind and won't obey the gospel (cf. Rev. 3:17). Suppose it rejects any call to holiness or to obedience in the area of social justice. In such churches the spiritual death, the principalities and powers, are not external but internal and real.

When vital faith and its components are reduced to traditional religion, when the church is content with the merely human, when the church is in bondage to the flesh, when the church is atheist in its practices even while claiming to have faith—then the destruction of the church is real. The Valley of Achor Church (or its corporate life and personality),[12] may sing gospel hymns and use orthodox words. It may buy into denominational programs and have a wonderful reputation (Rev. 2–3). But if it harbors the cancer of sin, it is deathly sick.

The Pauline teaching of the *flesh* (merely human, or fallen humanity) is important. I cannot blame Satan for my flesh or fallen nature. But again, Satan uses that fallen nature in the malignant chaos that is his domain, so I am in complicity with him. This is why Paul writes, "Do not give the devil a foothold" (Eph. 4:27).

We see congregations sit week after week in the pews and not see beyond sermons and sacraments to Monday morning. These rites are performed perfunctorily and sincerely but without causing a kingdom impact on our lives at 10:45 on Tuesday morning or at 3:50 on Thursday afternoon. The form has become the focus; the Word and the sacraments do not transform the church and the people. Theological experts may protest. But when congregational worship does not equip the participants to be scattered as "salt and light" in the Monday-morning world, the congregation is sick (Matt. 5:13-16).

Our struggle is with flesh and blood and with whatever energies seek to twist the world. "Submit yourselves, then, to God. Resist the devil, and he will flee from you" (James 4:7). "Be self-controlled and alert. Your enemy the devil prowls around like a roaring lion looking for someone to devour. Resist him, standing firm in the faith, because you know that your brothers throughout the world are undergoing the same kind of sufferings" (1 Pet. 5:8-9).

Literally, self-consciously, and verbally, we tell Satan that we know who he is. We submit ourselves again to God, renew our vows of faith in Jesus Christ, accept the authority of Holy Scriptures, and renounce and resist Satan, and claim victory in Christ.

> Be Thou my shield and hiding-place,
> that, sheltered neath thy side,
> I may my fierce accuser face,
> and tell him, "Thou has died." (John Newton, 1779)

To resist Satan is that and more. It does not mean that we are obsessed in some psychotic way with the presence and malice of Satan. To go back to Franz Overbeck, it means that the kingdom pastor becomes a witness against the pathology that binds the Valley of Achor Church in evil. That spiritual leader labors to replace pathology with the pattern on the mount. The kingdom pastor resists by positively affirming that in the resurrection of Christ, the new creation is turned loose in the world. "In Christ, there is a new creation: everything old has passed away; see, everything has become new!" (2 Cor. 5:17, NRSV).

After Constantine, the church sought to accommodate itself to this age of death and lost its alternative consciousness. It is called again by the kingdom pastor into kingdom consciousness, into its true calling, and into being sent out in daily mission.

To *resist* the devil means that we resist all that causes the church to inhabit spiritual death or lures it into evangelical amnesia. I recall the tragically humorous account from a pastor about a grande dame of his parish who effusively announced at tea, "I just love the Episcopal Church, . . . though I haven't believed in God for years!"

• • •

We discussed how this resistance differs in our churches. We asked, "How long does one resist?" We concluded that resisting the devil was basic to the ongoing task of the kingdom pastor.

• • •

To resist is to engage in patient ministry, calling the church back its eschatalogical self-awareness, to its otherness, to its alien status. Here, on the battlefield of the ages (1 Cor. 10:11, NRSV), between the advents of Christ, the kingdom pastor is called to be an overcomer and to evangelize the church afresh. How long should one labor in this work? Look at the Old Testament prophets such as Hosea who prophesied during the reign of king after king. So with us. This is no short-term project. It requires patience, gentleness, wisdom, and boldness.

The darkness and death take on personality and sneer at the kingdom pastor. They taunt him with the lie that they are unchangeable, that this is all there is, that the Valley of Achor is locked in. But God's promise is that if we resist the devil, "he will flee." The roaring lion is there but is not all he would have us believe he is! When we are on the side of Christ, the devil is the real loser.

The pathologies are real, and Satan is busy. The New Testament, Christ, and the apostles assume that. We are called to suffer with Christ if we are to reign with him (Luke 22:28-30; 2 Tim. 2:8-13). There is never any promise that Christ's victory will be exhibited in us without suffering (Luke 9:23-26; Col. 1:24). At the same time, we are assured that Christ is victorious. We can shout that Christ is risen! The struggles go on, but Christ has triumphed over death and hell. We are not called to shallow triumphalism but to the hope found in the resurrection. Hallelujah!

As we turn from the pathologies to the role of the kingdom pastor as the agent of God, we look at an ancient Christian hymn.

> Christian, dost thou see them on the holy ground, how the powers of darkness rage thy steps around? Christian, up and smite them, counting gain but loss [Phil. 3:7-8], in the strength that cometh by the holy cross. Well I know thy trouble, O my servant true, thou art very weary—I was weary too; but that toil shall make thee someday all Mine own, and the end of sorrow shall be near My throne.
>
> (ascribed to St. Andrew of Crete)

• • •

Andy closed with a prayer: "Father, I'm overwhelmed by all we've been looking at this evening. I'm not sure any of us are ready for the implications of what you have called us into. But thank you for time to reflect, to look again at what you will for us in your goodness—which we don't always understand.

"We end this day in praise. Thank you that you are always our mighty fortress. Though we have an ancient foe, that prince of hell, we thank you that we are not left to our own fragile resources but are given Christ Jesus. Bind us to him in the Spirit. Keep us in your grace and power. Deliver us from the evil one. Bring praise to your name as we offer ourselves to you as kingdom pastors, whatever that means. All praise to the Lamb of God. Amen."

7

Journey into Hope

IN CHAPTER ONE I let the giant waterbug illustrate the demonic power that sucks the insides out of many pastors. I introduced Ben, who represents pastoral seduction; Debbie, who represents pastoral frustration; and Andy, who represents pastoral resolution. They were ten years out of seminary and experiencing a poignant time at a conference. They realized that their original Vision of pastoral ministry (of a kingdom pastorate) had slipped further from their grasp. It all seemed so irreversible. . . . A little more of their insides had been sucked out.

Is it irreversible? We discussed that at our next gathering at a retreat center.

"Bob," Andy started, "I hope we're getting close to something beyond diagnosis. I need to know if all pastoral settings are irreversibly sick. Am I to become an empty skin floating on the water? Does God intend that? Do I hang onto my ordained status with clenched teeth and without any hope of change?"

"Yes, Bob," Ben added, "I'm not content to go on making my congregation or our congregations just an academic study. The folk in my congregation aren't just fictitious pawns in some game. They're my friends. They sincerely joined *something* they assumed was the Christian church. According to some confessional formulas, it is a church because God's Word is truly preached and the sacraments are truly administered. There is even a bit of discipline.

"I can see that critical elements of God's calling and mission are absent and unnoticed, but these are still real people! It's one thing for us to discuss missiology and ecclesiology in the abstract—but I need to deal with the reality of what I'm doing with these people!"

"Right. Achor and Hope are a good game," Debbie said, "but what do I *do,* given this understanding?"

So I began again, "I'm convinced that no congregation is beyond hope. I don't think God intends his pastors to clench their teeth and go on in grim resolve. Demanding questions need to be asked and tough issues faced. But Jesus says, 'I will build my church' [Matt. 16:18]."

Now I need to take some risks with my readers. I'm only one person who has struggled fallibly with these issues. From my own experience, I am sharing a moment of grace that transformed me from despair to hope; it underlies this entire book. I wouldn't be true to myself or to you if I didn't bear witness to it. In loftier theological terms and as a reminder of the Overbeck principle, I began to see my dismal pastoral setting with eschatological eyes. God's Vision lifted my pastoral setting above the civilization and culture of this spiritual death and gave me hope!

I can't explain how God speaks to his people, yet he does. I'm enough of a classical (even scholastic) Protestant to believe that the Scriptures are the only reliable and authoritative rule of faith and behavior. I'm leery of "voices" and the "inner light" of mystics. But I believe God communicates with his own. In the depths of my own hopelessness, thinking "How long, O Lord?" I was listening with strained ears for a Macedonian call into a more fulfilling and less painful pastorate.

I had a habit of taking long Saturday evening prayer walks in preparation for Sunday's ministry. Sundays were stressful, given the condition of the congregation. My walk took me through the heart of a working-class neighborhood, through the campus of a large university, and then to the sanctuary of our church building. I walked around inside the sanctuary in the dark, praying for the congregation. At that time my prayers were probably more for myself as a despairing pastor, with insides sucked out, than for the congregation.

I sat down on the left chancel steps. God asked me a startling question: *Do you believe I, even I, can revive, can bring life and reality to this congregation?*

Silent reflection. Then a bit hesitantly came my answer: "Yes."

Again God spoke. *If you can't trust me here, where it is humanly impossible, can you then trust me anywhere else? You could go to a more prominent place, or to a more congenial congregation, or to one that appears more humanly possible. But if you can't trust me to bring life here, how there? Where do I come into your understanding of your calling? Are you willing to stay here with me, in faithfulness, and see my purpose realized in this congregation?*

That was the last thing I wanted to hear. Again a long pause. I would have to trust God in the Valley of Achor, or forsake theological integrity and pastoral ministry. I didn't want to fake it for the rest of my days, proclaiming a God whom I really did not believe was capable. I made a decision with my stomach in my mouth. "Okay, Lord. Here I am, with you. Where do we begin?"

The theological question is critical. Are there congregations that are too much even for the sovereign God? Have they so inhabited the darkness that they are off-limits to the God of re-creating grace and mercy? Does God abandon his faithless and forgetful people? Does Satan have power to come into churches and possess the fickle people with religious death, then put up NO TRESPASSING signs to God, whose church and world this is? Does Satan whisper "hopeless" or "apostate" to the despairing pastor? Is the devil that is in the world greater than the Lord who is in us? (1 John 4:4).

I bear witness that I have met the risen Lord in the Valley of Achor. I have seen his faithfulness and his promises fulfilled. I testify to his good purpose, which is to create a Door of Hope in the most unlikely Valley of Achor, and so to bring praise to himself. My soul magnifies the Lord! So much is this so, that now in my personal pilgrimage (much closer to the end of my days), having pastored several fulfilling congregation, all my juices flow when I look at a congregation somebody has designated as "hopeless." I have a crazy conviction that God loves to surprise us with demonstrations of grace and power in unlikely places.

I do not believe this is a special apostolate or calling of mine, an aberration. If the Great Pastor, the Bishop and Shepherd of our souls (Heb. 13:20), came to seek and to save the lost, if God so loves the world that he gave his Son not to condemn but to save (John 3:16)—then the apparently dead and humanly hopeless congregations that still bear God's name are dear to his heart. Those congregations need kingdom pastors who have the Vision and the pattern given on the mount.

"Sounds good," declared Ben. "But is there a money-back guarantee?"

"I didn't say we always succeed. We may get terminated. We're not called to success but to faithfulness," I answered."

"Okay, but look at my situation. My congregation is

incredibly wealthy and comfortable. There is power and pride everywhere. That's not going to change. It's Laodicean down to its toenails [Rev. 3:14-22]. The Lord says that kind of church is pitiful, poor, blind, and naked. I struggle daily with the ethos of wealth. That's a different kind of hopelessness. And hey! There are a lot of perks in a church like that. It's not hard to take. But I often think I'm seduced beyond recovery. What does a kingdom pastor do in such a situation? Condemn it and stomp off? I can't believe that."

"I don't think it's that much different from other sicknesses of darkness," I replied. "In the Laodicea passage, look at the promise to such a church when it turns to God in repentance. That promise is the most extravagant one given to the seven churches in those accounts: 'I will give the right to sit with me on my throne, just as I overcame and sat down with my Father on his throne' [Rev. 3:21]. That tells me God longs for proud and prosperous congregations to come home to him, to true riches and fulfillment. The call is to be faithful in evangelizing such congregations while not becoming their captive."

There are tough issues to be faced as we journey into hope. The toughest is this: the darkness of this present age is malignant. It's no accident that it's called the *dominion* of Satan, of death. In the midst of this rebel dominion, the alternative dominion of God creates new communities, eschatalogical communities of the age to come. God calls these communities to be witnesses to the dominion of God's dear Son, to be model colonies of the kingdom of God.

However, these communities of the kingdom of God, these Door of Hope churches, within a generation tend to be subverted by the malignancy.[1] Soon churches forget their first love and become Valley of Achor congregations. They make wealth, success, efficiency, and power. They take their idols to the church and baptize them.

Enter kingdom pastors—who must be distinguished from clergy. Clergypersons may have doctor of ministry degrees, know their Myers-Briggs personality types, attend church-management seminars, and benefit from the best church-renewal institutes.[2] They may still not be equipped to be God's agents to create Hope in Achor. Clergy may be subverted and become chaplains to the darkness, ecclesiastical lapdogs, or keepers of the tribal rituals.[3] Clergy may be just incompetents who like the sound of "church vocation" and want to be called "reverend."

Yet Scripture, church, and history attest that kingdom pastors can be persons of modest gifts and still be touched by the grace of God. A kingdom pastor is an agent of hope, gospel, perseverance, faithfulness, and gentleness. A kingdom pastor is a reformer of the church and evangelist to the church. The kingdom pastor needs an enormous sense of humor born of robust faith in God's great salvation. She or he needs to be able to look at all of Satan's impossibilities, recognize their source, laugh, and say, "You gotta be kidding!"

"Don't you think you're overdoing it a bit?" Debbie asked. "It's hard to laugh when all hell is breaking loose! Biblical injunctions like 'Rejoice evermore!' or 'Give thanks at all times and in all occasions' don't help. But then, I don't like the alternative, going around under a cloud of gloom."

"I'm beginning to see that a lot of what I expected as a noble church professional wasn't based on the reality of clashing kingdoms," Andy said. "It would be pleasant to be just one more professional in a society of professionals. But you're showing us something more cosmic and conflictual. I think divinity schools could be charged with false advertising. It all looked so neat."

"Well, being a kingdom pastor sure looks more adventuresome and exciting than their promos," said Ben. "With this transformational dynamic in process, a guy couldn't get too bored, could he?"

Missionary to the Valley of Achor

Look at the mission field we're talking about here! There are thousands of Valley of Achor churches, the butt of jokes, making minimal impact, going through the motions. Yet most seminarians and pastors pray, "Lord, deliver me from such blight!" Who wants their insides sucked out? Still, here is this mission field of the humanly impossible congregations. They are church institutions, wineskins, in the middle of an increasingly unchurched, unevangelized, and secular populace.

Francis of Assisi, God's troubadour, began his remarkable career by rebuilding the Church of St. Damien out of ruins. There are many congregational and spiritual ruins today, with real people and remnants of grace. They need to be rebuilt into spiritual edifices, dwelling places for the Holy Spirit. Is this an exercise in masochism, a subtle self-destructive urge?

"Why not start new churches?" wondered Ben. "They're reputed to be a better way to reach the unreached. Why bother with churches that have become dysfunctional?"

Founding new congregations is a needed ministry but a different discipline. Even new churches have a life cycle and can soon become dysfunctional. New congregations face their own set of spiritual and practical hazards. This is not an either-or proposition. Creating Hope in Achor is as much a valid ministry as planting new kingdom communities. Our willingness to forsake existing congregations is disturbing. The church as eschatological community always exists in this battle behind the battle.

Donald Jacobs, a Mennonite theologian, says,

> Jesus Christ laid out the problem in its stark dimensions. He recognized the rule of Satan over societies and the willful disobedience of our race. It was into this hostile milieu that Jesus came, God in human flesh. Rejected, he confided in his disciples, "If the world hates you, keep in mind that it hated me first. If you belonged to the world, it would love you as its own. As it is, you do not belong to the world, but I have chosen you out of the world. That is why the world hates you" (John 15:18-19). Every believing community, he insisted, lives its life in an essentially unfriendly environment because Christians are players in the cosmic spiritual battle in which the forces of evil are intent on drawing people away from God. This spiritual conflict undergirds every act, thought, and teaching of Jesus Christ and the apostles.[4]

Let's get on with the pragmatics of our ministry. Satan's power is real and ongoing. The battle between the beast and Lamb is with us. Is there a way to overcome? To renew? To rebuild? To build and to plant? Yes.

> They overcame [the accuser] by the blood of the Lamb, and by the word of their testimony; they did not love their lives so much as to shrink from death. (Rev. 12:11)

The triumph of Calvary is real, but the spiritual battle goes on. It is fascinating to be living at this moment. The presence and activity of God's church in the world defies theological scholasticism and imagination. In many parts of the two-thirds world, the church is growing with phenomenal speed and power amid the most adverse circumstances. In settings of oppression, opposition, and deprivation, the church is alive, joyous, and faithful. Out of the turmoil of the former communist bloc, the church is emerging as a vital factor in the cause of evangelism, peace, and justice. Christians are overcomers and have hope in the midst of blight. "Glory in the church and in Christ Jesus." Amen.

However, we are here, not there! The purpose of our fabricated Door of Hope paradigm is to convey the vision of God's glory in the community of the age to come. In our setting, that integrity is rare. By faith the kingdom pastor *always* sees the Door of Hope in the Valley of Achor. He is always a Door of Hope pastor and always excited. She is filled with inexpressible joy because of a theology of cross and resurrection. She knows that in her Valley of Achor, the church in its God-given intent is *humanly impossible.* The kingdom pastor understands by faith that the Door of Hope is *always* there.

Your ministry always takes place where you *are,* not where you're *not.* Just as the apostle John walked on the isle of Patmos with Jesus, so you walk in Achor with the ascended Lord. It is always impossible for humans, yet always in process with God (Luke 18:27).

The church where you now are is a composite of the seven churches in Asia Minor described in Revelation 2–3. Your church is always a mixture of faith and faithlessness. But as a kingdom pastor, you are there with the Vision, the pattern given on the mount. You have the power of the resurrection; the Door of Hope is there *in you.* The risen Christ walks *with you* amid sufferings and in your unlikely setting. You become Christ's evangelist to his church.[5] The church must be reevangelized in every generation. A gospel hymn states it plainly:

> Tell me the old, old story. . . .
> Tell me the story often,
> for I forget so soon;
> The early dew of morning
> Has passed away at noon. (Catherine Hankey)

As a kingdom pastor, you intercede before Christ on behalf of the Vision. There is that boundary path, Forsyth explains,[6] between this age and the age to come. On that border we walk with our risen Lord in the incredible ministry of intercession, to pray into reality that which we know of his will. We hold the Vision before the Lord who calls it into being. Prayer! Forgotten weapon in our arsenal (Eph. 6:10-18).

We become Christ's resident agents of hope. These three roles, *evangelist, intercessor,* and *agent of hope,* are intertwined. The Vision is not of a rich church (rich churches come off badly in Scripture), a successful church (likewise),[7] or a super-church. The gospel of the kingdom is addressed to the poor, the crushed, the blind, and the imprisoned. It reaches out to real sinners, to nobodies, to the helpless, despairing, and empty. The gospel is addressed to a church marked by the cross, a church that dies to its own life so others might live. Only then is the church truly the body of Christ. The calling is not to success, but to faithfulness, spiritual health, and growth. Hope emerges out of Achor.

Prosperous churches face particular hazards. Mammon is the major competitor for the worship of God's people, according to the Gospels (Matt. 6:24). North America is filled with prosperous churches. The kingdom pastor must help such congregations to see the stewardship and ministry of such seductive wealth.[8] Idolatry of denomination is also seductive in mainline churches. Idolatry of nation is often enthroned in conservative and evangelical churches. Nobody escapes the tendency toward idolatry. All idols corrupt the integrity of God's community.

The waiting Lord Jesus wants to reenter his church (Rev. 3:20). He wants to be welcomed again into his people's heart, to sit again at table in intimate communion. That's the Vision, the glory, the joy.

Contracting and Agenda Sharing

"All well and good," Debbie noted. "But what about the flip side? I've still got a congregation with a corporate mentality of Achor, Bob. I don't mean that to sound ominous, but face it! The way you describe the Vision of us kingdom pastors is probably light-years from where most garden-variety North American congregations are located. We've got a communication problem, or we'll be getting more insides sucked out."

"You really are a nuts-and-bolts type, Debbie!" I exclaimed. "But you're right on target. That delicate task of communicating the Vision is essential. This journey into hope must not remain a mystery to the congregation; it must be the first step in the evangelizing process. We are called to tell what God has showed us and to be witnesses to that hope. Let's work on that process."

My denomination has pulpit committees or pastoral search committees. A pastor can talk and negotiate with significant and elected members of the church before being called. She can ask questions, share kingdom agenda, and contract with the committee before the call is issued. The negative side is that distressingly few committees are ready to face creativity, newness, and change. Yet this is the group charged with facilitating the call to a pastor.

In an episcopal system, pastors are appointed by their bishop, though parishes usually have a committee to negotiate with the bishop and interview the appointee. Early in their tenure, pastors in an episcopal system must meet with the church council and other significant people to process the Vision. The point is not to overwhelm them with your agenda, but to ask questions about their appraisal, their vision, and their hopes. Then tell them your story of faith and discipleship, your understanding of the gospel of the kingdom of God, your kingdom agenda, and your sense of kingdom pastorate.

One effective pastor used such a procedure in one-on-one lunch meetings with the effective leaders in the church. The setting contributed to quiet disciple making and Vision building.

This approach will be new to folk who have had only custodial pastors. Valley of Achor has drifted so far from any sense of *calling*-ecclesiology, or of *sending*-missiology that some will not understand this approach. But even negative reactions can be a blessing. The pastor can process reasons and assumptions behind the reaction.

Accepting a call to a Valley of Achor church is not submission to masochism or self-destruction. If a pastor *needs* a call so much that he or she forsakes any kingdom principle, that pastor has a problem. A pastor must not be so eager to receive a call that he or she is for sale at any price. At the same time, a congregation without integrity should not "hire" a new preacher.

It is important to know each other's stories and agendas. The pastor must know the church's story, traditions, hurts, disappointments, joys, accomplishments, and dreams. Who are the saints, the good and exemplary folk? Who are the influential people, even if quiet and not in leadership positions? How willing are these people to go through the pain of growth and change, even of *life,* which comes by the Spirit? Who are the Annas and Simeons (Luke 2) who long for and pray for the coming salvation?

It is important to be straightforward with pastoral search committees, for their sake as well as the pastor's. If one or both parties are unwilling to lay agendas on the table, there is conflict. I need to know (or want to know) what these folk understand about me and what attracted them to me. The answers are not always heartening! They often don't know much, even in the best of circumstances.

Perhaps someone gave them my name or they heard I was available. That's okay. Such committees tend to be pragmatic; the congregation elected them to find a pastor, so that's what they do. They're not always philosophical. Many congregations fill out a congregational information form, which is supposed to make them think through their life and mission. However, committees don't always use that study in finding a pastor.

Still, I like these conversations. They are fun and educational. If I were ecclesiastically ambitious and courting a larger church, I might be more anxious. That has never been my style. I'm always amazed when, as consultant to or candidate at prestige churches, I meet with sincere but inept committees. Committee members with responsible positions in their professions nevertheless tend not to ask basic questions about the church or the pastoral ministry. For this reason, I love to ask questions, right down to the skeletons-in-the-closet question: What is there about this congregation that you do *not* want me to know?

If I am called to lead this congregation on the journey into hope, I want as much mutual understanding as possible, especially since that journey involves the warfare between the Lamb and the beast. I want to be a person of genuineness, gentleness, sensitivity, and pastoral Vision! That has risks. I must be free to accept or reject their call. I must also be willing to be rejected or called. If a bishop assigned me, the same principles would prevail, but the choice would not be mine to make.

It is crucial to have a clear and written contract as to what the church expects and what I agree to be and do. The contract reminds me and the pastoral relations group that I am accountable to what our agreement is. Then I am less vulnerable to every person imposing his or her agenda on me as months and years go by.

Andy protested, "But it still sounds idealistic. Just

what percentage of churches we deal with are able to resonate with the Vision we're talking about? My experience is that the committee is usually focused on logistics like availability, salary, and schedules. You're talking about the lofty principles of God's purpose."

"Let me share a conviction. I believe that as the cultural setting around us grows more secularized and as darkness more and more inhabits the church, pastors need a back-up profession, a tent-making trade, so we don't *need* a pastorate to survive economically. If a pastor *must* have the call, it's too easy to sell out theological convictions."

"I wonder what these laypersons on the committee come with," Ben said. "I wonder what image they have of clergy. I wonder if they have hidden and genuine expectations of a pastor who will bring them into living relationship with Christ, a pastor who is genuinely and deeply Christian, not just a church professional enhancing a career. Did you ever wonder that? It's so easy to be selfishly focused on ourselves that we don't hear their heartbeat."

Ben put his finger on a dimension not often recognized, especially by clergy. It's critical that we as kingdom pastors understand that the church is the *laity*. For so long in Christendom, including in our seminaries, the church has seemed to exist for the clergy. But God's people, God's *laos,* make up more than 95 percent of the church. This community of people is summoned by God to be the living demonstration of the new creation. That is the church's reason for existing.

Pastors are called to equip and facilitate the mission of God through this community. Our faithfulness is not measured by how popular or successful we are in creating a remarkable sermon, leading a worship service, or working in a church institution. We are faithful if we use our skill in Scripture and prayer to equip members to be effective agents of the new creation in the 160 and more hours each week they spend scattered as salt and light.

This should be discussed in the initial meetings with pulpit committees and church leadership. A church focused on the laity and their Monday morning work will capture the imagination of thoughtful and serious Christians. It is the wave of the future. This is a different image than we have lived with for centuries, and certainly different from what laity have come to expect of clergy. While we clergy go about our clergy stuff, many laypeople are hungry to know how to relate their Christian faith to their daily lives. They are frustrated by clergy preoccupation with church programs.[9]

Many pastors minister in a stupor; that is a manifestation of spiritual conflict. They almost blindly retreat from one Valley of Achor church to another—or move up to more prominent churches, which may be the same thing. They never see the emergence of the Door of Hope, never see men and women mature into discipleship, conscious of being servants of the new creation, the kingdom of God. Often the most conscientious are most easily discouraged with rigid congregations, have their insides sucked out, and seek escape. All of us have a streak of Jonah in us. We're willing in theory to be God's prophets, but not in this particular Nineveh.

The journey into hope is a journey into the unknown, into pain and joy. It is a journey into the Vision with the risen Christ. We also "participate in the sufferings of Christ" (1 Peter 4:13; 2 Cor. 1:5; Col. 1:24). The journey begins with the kingdom pastor gently sharing the Vision with those who will be along on the journey.

"It is certainly easy to get seduced into something less than the Vision, isn't it?" said Debbie. "How do we keep our eyes clear and our heart in tune?"

Nothing is more important than making our lives be the incarnation of genuineness or clarity. Like Jesus in the hymn of Philippians 2, we need to be incarnations of humility and mission faithfulness. That begins with daily time with the Lord in the disciplines of Word and prayer. We need that time with God to process all we're involved with, the spiritual, theological, missiological, and communal dimensions. We must be refined in the presence of the Holy One. Kingdom pastors need to be created in holiness. That doesn't take place if we are too busy for quiet time with the Holy God. Daily we need to be reminded of God's love, the mystery of God's workings, and of our own vulnerability.[10] Otherwise we let the Vision grow dim or distorted.

Prayer and the Journey into Hope

I see my role as a kingdom pastor as one who sculpts the Door of Hope out of the Valley of Achor material. My tools are the *Word of God* and *prayer*. I will discuss the Word in another chapter. Here I want to register the basic place of prayer in the work of the kingdom pastor. In Acts 6 the apostles stated the necessity of giving their attention to prayer and the ministry of the Word. That was no accident. In God's good purpose for the church, someone has to have clear Vision. That person must stand before God, with God, and in God to call that Vision into reality.

In earlier chapters we dealt with the community of the Great King and the pattern given on the mount. That becomes the stuff of prayer. "Thy will be done!" We confess who we are amid all the realities of the Valley of Achor, the persons and the developing spiritual character of the congregation, which the Revelator calls the "angel of the church."[11] We then pray the Word and the gospel of the kingdom into reality, perseveringly and urgently.

Prayer is work. Forsyth says, "It is a wrestle on the greatest scale—all manhood taxed as in some great war, or some great negotiation of state. And the effect is exhaustion often. No, the result of true prayer is not always peace." [12] We pastors invoke Acts 6 when we don't want to "serve tables" but are not so diligent in the crucial ministry of Word and prayer. Prayer is learned by praying.

Thirty years ago, long before I heard of "prayer journaling," I took a spiral-bound notebook and began recording prayer concerns, pertinent Scriptures, and prayer requests. This went on casually page after page, month after month. Somewhere along the way, I began to write whole prayers instead of just notes. The patterns began to emerge in prayer as the Vision of the Door of Hope took form from my study of the Word and existential involvement as a kingdom pastor. Prayers of exalted vision, prayers of despair, prayers of agony, prayers of elation and thanksgiving—just like the Psalms!

I have many stenographic pads of these prayers. It is a fascinating exercise for me now to reread them. It took me a long time to realize that God was answering those prayers. God was praying through me. The real outbreakings of life and hope were not the result of my outstanding personality or dynamic preaching (vanity!); they were the result of out-of-sight prayer, month in and month out. Through that prayer, God formed me as a kingdom pastor and formed the church into the Door of Hope.

The "whole armor of God" passage in Ephesians is a resource in the war between the dominion of Satan and the reign of God's Son. It concludes with a call to prayer.

> Pray in the Spirit on all occasions with all kinds of prayers and requests. With this in mind, be alert and always keep on praying for all the saints. Pray also for me, that whenever I open my mouth, words may be given me so that I will fearlessly make known the mystery of the gospel, for which I am an ambassador in chains. Pray that I may declare it fearlessly, as I should. (Eph. 6:18-20)

The destructive forces are real. But a faithful Savior provides the armor and spiritual weapons. Prominent in this armory is prayer, given so we may "stand" in the "day of evil" (6:13).

Look at the opening of the seventh seal in Revelation.

> When he opened the seventh seal, . . . another angel, who had a golden censor, came and stood at the altar. He was given much incense to offer, with the prayers of all the saints, on the golden altar before the throne. The smoke of the incense, together with the prayers of the saints, went up before God from the angel's hand. Then the angel took the censor, filled it with fire from the altar, and hurled it on the earth; and there came peals of thunder, rumblings, flashes of lightning and an earthquake. (Rev. 8:1, 3-5)[13]

The prayers of God's people determine the journey of the congregation and the history of the world. "The intercession of Christ in heaven is the continuity and consummation of his supreme work on earth. To share it is the meaning of praying in the Spirit. And it has more effect on history than civilization has."[14] The kingdom pastor needs to excel in the discipline of intercessory prayer in which the Word of God, the heart of God, and the power of God are engaging and transforming pastor and congregation.

There are loaded promises given to prayers offered in groups, when believers agree to ask God for the mercies of his saving, renewing purpose. You'll probably not find a lot of takers in the Valley of Achor. Prayer is intimidating to the merely human (carnal) members. But if you do get a lot of takers, rejoice. Things are better than you thought. When one or two others covenant to pray with you, you can help others into prayer as they help you and the church into hope.

My experience is that such groups are not dramatic but enormously fruitful. I am uneasy about super-saints who sail off into eloquent prayers; they claim all kinds of authority and intimidate quiet people who come modestly but faithfully to the Father with requests.

Once I gave a blanket invitation to a group of men to join me on Friday mornings for breakfast and prayer. I think some were more interested in pleasing the new pastor and eating the restaurant food than in prayer. But five or six turned up. It was an opportunity to meet some great people, begin to communicate prayers, equip for prayer, and pray with others.

Along the way, one man's wife joined, and soon others began to participate. We moved it to the church building. Every Friday morning year after year, ordinary good folk, enjoying one another and God, prayed all kinds of prayers from modest petitions for the sick to strategic kingdom prayers for the journey into hope. How faithful is our Lord! There were other groups also praying. That ministry of prayer was a key to understanding what God was doing in opening the Door of Hope for our community.

When I speak on the disciplines of church renewal, I tend to tell the more obvious and visible things I have learned in my journey from Achor to Hope. Then my wife reminds me, "You didn't mention prayer." She's right. I'm learning. Without prayer in the Spirit, there will not likely be any Door of Hope in the Valley of Achor. The church wedded to this present age of death doesn't see any need for prayer. But the church that sees itself as part of the colony of the age to come will know the urgency of the ministry of prayer. "Pray without ceasing."

• • •

"I'm caught off base here," Andy admitted. "I love to read and reflect, but I've never been disciplined to understand or practice prayer as a priority. Oh, we have those printed liturgical prayers in the books. And I know there are many evangelical writings extolling the importance of prayer. But as part of the sculpting ministry and the critical and life-giving part of our ministry—well, I just never wakened up to this.

"We need to pray now," Andy continued, "but I've got another suggestion. I'd like to enter into a prayer covenant with the three of you for thirty days. I want to give myself to God with the prayer that he'll teach me prayer and show me how to pray as a pastor. I want to pray the same for you. Let's pray that God will create us by his Spirit into kingdom pastors and reveal the ministry of prayer in the most wholesome and effective way. I need this. Are you guys up to it? Let's just get going in prayer. This is a first step."

All agreed. We held hands, prayed for each other, and committed ourselves to the thirty-day prayer covenant.

8

Overcoming: Sculpting the Vision

IT HAD been nearly a year since my three friends had met at the conference and shared their loss of Vision. We were near the end of our agreed-upon time for meetings. I reminded the three of them of their original dilemma and of the ground we covered in seeking to come to grips with the spiritual conflict over pastoral ministry.

"Does it occur to you," Ben said, "that those who purportedly equipped us for ministry left out a few key points? [Laughter]. They didn't tell us about the dimension of the clashing kingdoms."

"Yes," agreed Debbie. "And maybe I'm too conformed to Enlightenment thinking, but why consign all this stuff to Satan? Is it more than just ordinary human foibles?"

"Yes and no!" I replied. "Yes, we can never blame Satan for the fruit of our merely human nature. The New Testament describes the destructive behavior patterns of our flesh *in the church*. But it also speaks of a *kosmos* (world) in the power of the wicked one. That evil one is the 'spirit who is now at work in those who are disobedient' [Eph. 2:2]."

What energizes this destructive, malignant, and persistent behavior in the individuals and structures of society? It is not neutral out there. The dominion of God breaks into the dominion of Satan. We have a difficult time with that concept. Paul deals with our anger, then exhorts us: "Do not give the devil a foothold" (Eph. 4:26-27). Such linkages crop up all through the New Testament, such as in the Lord's Prayer: "Deliver us from the evil one."

There are other reminders. A friend was flying from the West Coast. His seatmate bowed his head in prayer. My gregarious Christian friend said, "Oh, are you a Christian? I saw that you were praying."

The seatmate responded, "No, I'm a Satanist. I was praying for the destruction of Christian clergy."

Is the book of Revelation a true account of the cosmic conflict? In her call to face the destructive supernatural forces that oppose the missionary enterprise, Neuza Itioka comments,

> For too long the Western church has tended toward an intellectual expression of its faith, failing to face realistically the supernatural manifestations it must confront. . . . The rational intellectual approach we have used for so long brings only new information, a new way of thinking. What we need to reach people who co-exist daily with the supernatural is the powerful presence of the risen Christ.[1]

We must take much more seriously the scriptural teaching concerning this evil age and its ramifications. But I now want to focus on more normal pastoral functions which are nevertheless played out against the background of overcoming in this conflict. We need a positive note.

• • •

The human impossibility of the calling of the kingdom pastor is what makes it so thrilling—like Isaiah's desert which rejoices and blossoms and shouts for joy (Isa. 35:1-2)! Crazy? Impossible? Yes! That is probably why we have tended to reduce the church and the gospel of the kingdom to something more humanly achievable, to make evangelism a marketing technique. Within this impossible dominion of darkness is also a destructive personality that is within the providence of God and for our sanctification.[2] It can become unnerving!

"Sounds like we're back to Overbeck," Andy said. "We've drawn Christianity into the sphere of civilization, right? So we've been snookered by Satan, denying the essentially eschatological character of the Christian religion. Not a bad assessment, huh?"

"One response is paranoia," I explained, "seeing conflict in every interruption of our plans and Satan always present. Satan magnifies himself while he obscures the work of Christ; he frequently drives God's people into joyless defensiveness. The call to be joyfully engaged in the battle and to sing the song of Moses and the Lamb doesn't make sense in that frame of mind."

Oswald Chambers uses the metaphor of the difference between surfers and nonswimmers facing a high surf. To the nonswimmer, the surf is sheer terror; to the surfer, it is life's ecstasy. The satanic challenges to the kingdom pastor are high surf indeed. Paranoia? Or adventure into joy?

I see the challenge of the Vision as a legitimate biblical and implementable goal. However, it is not likely that God will pour out much of his Holy Spirit on a community still full of cultural, economic, political, social, and personal idolatries that grieve and quench the Spirit. It is not sufficient to say "Lord, Lord" with impeccable orthodoxy while in practice keeping our idols in place. Nor is it enough to be pentecostal and to speak in unknown tongues if there is no kingdom-shaped discipleship that demonstrates the Holy Spirit and power.

North American Christianity has learned how to speak gospel words and live pagan lives. Liberal and evangelical Christians are equally guilty. In the name of one brand of orthodoxy, they point at the bad doctrine and sins of *others* but are blind to how they themselves are possessed by idols, especially mammon. How's that for high surf? It is the context of the church in which we all live.

"Spell some of that out," Ben suggested. "It sounds like you're saying most of us are guilty of some kind of Christian Faith Lite."

"Yes," I agreed, "Gospel Lite is not a bad way of putting it. In its purity the New Testament message is offensive to normal ways of living and thinking. Some want to make it palatable and surgically slice out a point that offends. Ellul calls that *elision*.[3] In trendy programs, even denominational agencies do this (as Debbie has noted)."

If that is not enough to raise anxiety, examine the many things we assume in the church: that (1) members of the church are Christian, (2) visible members are disciples, (3) members are joined to become part of the community of the kingdom of God, (4) the leadership of the church has some sense of what is going on spiritually, (5) the Bible and the church's theology is known and determines things, (6) the congregation's experience with pastors is positive and a new leader is received without suspicion, and (7) you (the pastor) know what you're doing and why God has sent you there.

High surf? But there is good news, a word from God! It's not new. I'm saying it against the backdrop of the battle behind the battle. Paul is aware of that hidden battle and is sure of the outcome for believers: "The God of peace will soon crush Satan under your feet" (Rom. 16:20).

Revelation is a wonderful pastoral book in which the risen Lord Jesus meets the apostle John in a prison colony called Patmos. The Lord assures John that he walks in the midst of his church, represented by the golden lampstands. That means Christ is with us in whatever Patmos or Valley of Achor we find ourselves.

The whole writing is in the context of worship, from the apostle "in the Spirit on the Lord's day," to the myriads in heaven singing, "Worthy is the Lamb that was slain!" The letters to the angels of the seven churches reveal that several of them are sliding toward the Valley of Achor. We catch scenes on earth and scenes in heaven that help us understand our life as the Lamb's church. Revelation is pastoral through and through.

To those kingdom pastors looking for a clue, turn to Revelation 12:11. Concerning the ongoing conflict between the Lamb and the beast, the woman and the dragon, John says, "They overcame him by *the blood of the Lamb* and by *the word of their testimony;* they did not love their lives so much as to shrink from death."

Note three things. First, the saints have overcome by the blood of the Lamb. Second, their overcoming includes the word of their testimony. Third, they did not love their lives so much that they shrank from death.

As the kingdom pastor desires to overcome, to sculpt the church in Word and prayer, here is Christ's guide to integrity! It includes the focus and authority of Jesus, the Lamb of God, and his blood of the new covenant. The content of our labors is the Word of Christ as set forth in apostolic writings, incarnated in our lives as kingdom pastors, and spoken to church and world.

In familiar liturgical figures, our resources are (1) the bread and wine of the Lord's Supper, "my body, my blood of the covenant for the remission of sins"; (2) the preaching of the Word of God, the word of the cross; and (3) the waters of baptism, "buried with him in his death, . . . raised to live a new life." The Lord's Supper (eucharist), preaching of the Word of God, and baptism must always be sculpting, overcoming instruments. Since these may become trivialized and reduced to empty rites, let us look at their content. They become central ministries and must not be truncated. They must be the kingdom pastor's flesh and bone, incarnated in the pastor's life, before they can model, teach, and sculpt the congregation.

The Blood of the Lamb

In John's writings, the blood of the Lamb speaks all that is gathered up in the life, death, and resurrection of Christ, yet it focuses on the cross and the atonement. Paul says that the cross is foolishness to the Greeks—and so it is to our culture. In Revelation 5, the apostle John wept because no one was found to open the sealed scroll. Then one elder pointed him to the Lion of Judah, who had triumphed and was able to open the scroll. When John turned, instead of a lion, he saw a Lamb looking as if it had been slain, standing in the place of authority.

A slain Lamb! That makes our Christian gospel so radical. When the eternal Son came into his profaned creation as the incarnation of God, he rewrote the agenda. To be rich is to be poor, to be great is to be servant, to live is to die, to be strong is to be weak. In his case, to be vulnerable, despised, and executed on a cross was to become Savior of sinners and Lord of all.

The Lamb slain is the Lion of Judah. The world and much of the church don't understand the Lamb, the Lamb's true followers, the Lamb's agenda, and the cross. We keep trying to reduce faith to religion or ethical precepts. We romanticize the Sermon on the Mount, with its upside-down teachings. But Paul preached Christ crucified. The overcomers conquered the dragon with the blood of the Lamb.

The Roman empire and the Jerusalem establishment sought to rid themselves of the troublesome Lamb. But they found that they hadn't destroyed him. They had only enabled him to redefine power. The executioner's gallows became Christ's triumph, from which true power flows. "Having disarmed the powers and authorities, [Christ] made a public spectacle of them, triumphing over them by the cross" (Col. 2:15).

That is only a beginning. The cross is fathomless in its meaning, a "never-ending treasury." By the shedding of the Lamb's blood, the new and everlasting covenant was ratified on the cross. The once-for-all atonement for sins was made. The kingdom of God was inaugurated and validated. Consciences were and are being cleansed from dead works to serve the living God. The cross and the resurrection are the death of death. By the blood of the cross, peace is made between heaven and earth. Reconciliation between the offended Creator and the offending creatures is sealed. The old has passed away; the new creation has come (2 Cor. 5:17).

The Lamb slain is the real power and authority. Defeat is victory. "This is my body, which is for you. . . . This cup is the new covenant in my blood. . . . Whenever you eat this bread and drink this cup, you proclaim the Lord's death until he comes" (1 Cor. 11:23-26). Here is the heart of our faith.

However, this present age of death is running with *dragons*, not *lambs*! It still blindly deals with concepts of power, wealth, prestige, and self-fulfillment—all of which have been made invalid by the Lamb and the cross. The kingdom of darkness and of Satan keeps flailing away, even though its power is broken and its defeat sealed by the blood of the Lamb.

The Valley of Achor Church forgets this and allows evil to come in, with its affinity for the dragon, and relegates the Lamb and his blood to an obscure corner. "And if the light that is in you be darkness, how great is that darkness!" (Matt. 6:23). Current therapeutic preaching isn't against the atonement; it just doesn't bother to mention it. The kingdom pastor moves the cross, the blood of the Lamb, and the atonement back to center stage.

Therefore we confess and believe that Satan and the dominion of death are defeated. Yet the risen Lord has called his faithful pastors to the battlefield between the ages, and this is a dangerous ministry. The cross radically redefines our individual lives and also politics, economics, history, power, priorities, justice, militarism, and all of corporate life and thought. And the angry dragon has teeth!

> For I resolved to know nothing while I was with you except Jesus Christ and him crucified (1 Cor. 2:2).

The Word of Their Testimony

The Word of Christ dwells richly in the kingdom pastor (Col. 3:16), and through her that word of Christ is to become the common mind of the congregation. Yet seminarians and congregations often do not put a high priority on a pastor's skill in preaching from the Scriptures. However, the kingdom pastor should diligently cultivate skill in biblical exposition.

"Bob, do you have suggestions for cultivating such skill?" prodded Debbie.

Skilled preachers spend time daily being formed and transformed by Scripture. Such preachers study, reflect, search, pray, practice, and exercise the full range of their minds to hone their skills. More significant biblical scholarship has been printed since the end of World War II than earlier. This is available to all. Models of expository preachers are harder to find, but those who are models dwell deeply and daily in Scripture, seeking not more knowledge but God.

I read widely in biblical studies. In unexpected places, some writer cleans the dust out of my filters and gives me an understanding that sets me free to go further. But forming the common mind of the congregation according to the Word of God is more easily said than done. Sculpting is slow work. A good part of the church in this land dwells in abysmal ignorance of Scriptures. In effect, churches have edited their documents to delete any clear sense of mission,[4] urgency, discipleship, and costly obedience to Christ. Thus it is no surprise that many pastors have no vision of God's intention for the congregation.

Where do we start? An African pastor at a missionary training institute in Texas heard the leaders pussyfooting around the missionary task. Finally he could contain himself no longer. "You folk in the church here have a failure of nerve at the point of conversion, don't you?" Conversion is needed: repentance, holiness, and turning from idolatry.

Jacques Ellul argues that Christianity in the West has been subverted. The task is now "to subvert the subversion."[5] That's what overcoming "by the word of their testimony" is all about (Rev. 12:11). It's going to take time! It's going to take deliberate, intentional, and transformational efforts that require conflict, suffering, much intercession, change, some people leaving.[6] Count on five to ten years to begin to bring into being a true *ek-klēsia* (called-out people) of the kingdom of God, a Door of Hope Church, with the alternative consciousness necessary for kingdom community.

Zealous pastors (especially young ones) never like to hear that five-to-ten-year news. "If it doesn't happen in six months, forget it!" There may be instant evangelistic awakenings, but that's a category different from a congregation in which the word of Christ dwells richly (Col. 3:16). Such strong, wholesome Door-of-Hope congregations require pastors to take time, lots of time, to labor in the Word—and to sweat!

This skill in the Word is strategic and critical in carrying out God's mission in the world. We see in the New Testament that the church becomes distracted and ill-focused. When the early church had to provide for widows, the apostles affirmed that the church must meet those needs. But they also placed priority on their own ministry of Word and prayer (Acts 6). Why? Because God gives that gift to keep the church's Vision and mission clear.

At a concert of the Atlanta Symphony, my wife commented on the role of the concertmaster. Before the concert and after intermission, she made sure that the orchestra was in tune and on key. That is the role the pastor and teacher is to have according to Ephesians 4. This pastor is a gift of God and gifted by the Spirit to equip all God's people for their particular ministry in the gospel. The pastor is to see that they are mature, not buffeted about by every intellectual, cultural, moral, and spiritual wind that blows (Eph. 4:11-13).

"Bob, a point of clarification, please," said Ben. "Exactly what area are we seeking to sculpt in the individual lives of our members? I can see the Vision given on the mount insofar as the congregation is concerned. But the congregation is made up of individuals called Christians. They're the components of this larger vision. Clarify what we're working toward."

We're working by Word and Spirit to see Christ formed in these men and women (cf. Gal. 4:19). Later we will discuss *disciple-making*. Paul consistently taught us that believers are a new creation being formed into the likeness of Christ (Rom. 8:29). That means individual Christians and the Christian community are to have faith like Christ's, think like Christ, obey like Christ, will to do the Father's will as Christ does, and know the Father as Christ does. Communities and individuals are to be the glory of God as sons and daughters of the Father.

This process (sanctification) is never complete. That is why the sculpting by Word is essential. It is also one reason why there is so often pressure to "do this later" or to preempt the priority for something more pressing. Demonic? Perhaps. It means also that the process must be obvious in us pastors, so we can be models of what we teach and sculpt. Pastor-teachers are both mentors and models.

My youngest son, Danny, was a world-class 10,000-meter runner. In his strenuous training days, he spoke of "base-building." That meant developing superb conditioning from which he could push himself to almost superhuman effort when necessary. Base-building was a disciplined, day-in-and-day-out grind. It was made bearable only by the vision of success in future meets.

The kingdom pastor has to do *base-building* in the knowledge and understanding of Scriptures. Devotional tidbits or spiritualized Bible stories will not do. The congregation must do base-building in the Word of Christ.

Caution! This base-building, "word of their testimony" ministry has risks. Other gospels in and out of the church are real and resist challenge. When real disciple-making is taking place, when the gospel of the dominion of God is nurtured, Christ has totalitarian claim on our lives. This is alien to the gospel of the *Wall Street Journal, Better Homes and Gardens*, the Democratic Party, the Republican Party, social agendas, church growth, the fast lane, the secret lodge, capitalism, or any other ism.

All will try (and often succeed) to make the gospel of the kingdom support or express their gospel. When exposed, all hell (literally) can break loose. The "Great Whore Babylon," that metaphor of Revelation 17–18, has many ways to express seductions, including religion!

"Time out!" Andy cried. "That's about enough for the moment. I'm beginning to see patterns and hands-on stuff I've got to deal with. But enough for one session! Let's take a break for lunch."

"Right. We'll pick up here when we continue this afternoon."

9

Disciple-making, Preaching, Cross-bearing

AS WE walked around after lunch, Andy reflected, "I love spending time searching Scripture, and I love trying to preach it. But I wonder if I'm constructing a world of my own that has little to do with the lives of my people."

"When I went to seminary out of my brief business career," Ben said, "I felt it was another world. The things we dealt with and fussed about in seminary were not the things that occupied me as a Christian in the business world."

"Right!" Debbie confirmed. "After some of the traumas of teaching school, given all the stresses of education in this society, seminary was an escape for me. I was relieved to be living in the subculture of theological reflection, without the demands of teaching the public."

A devastatingly effective though clandestine strategy of the darkness is making such a formal clergy office out of the ministry of the Word and of the church.[1] *Disciple-*

making is a key to keeping the focus on the laity. In seminary, students join the *clergy subculture*. They see through clergy eyes and forget the true purpose of the pastor-teacher gift. This skewed perspective tends to follow most clergy all their careers. While they accomplish much good work, it blinds them to the Vision of God's purpose among all of God's people, the laity.

• • •

The kingdom pastor sees all life through the spectacles of Scripture and sees all Scripture missiologically. The kingdom pastor must also see all that he or she does *through the eyes of the laity*. The kingdom pastor remembers that as the *church gathered*, it is most visible; but members must be equipped to live as God's priests and faithful witnesses where they are for most of the week. Unless we do that, what we do inside the gathered community is part of the darkness!

Disciple-making

Large institutional churches focused on clergy, pulpits, and preaching have subverted a focus on Scripture which must be reclaimed. In Ephesians 4:11-13, the apostle states that the ascended Lord gives to his church the gift of pastor-teachers. Their role is *to equip God's folk for their ministries* and to bring them to maturity in Christ. Even more compelling, the pastor is to bring the laity to the "whole measure of the fullness of Christ." God's people are not to languish in childish immaturity, tossed back and forth by every threat in their life setting.

That Ephesians passage looks at the product of the *ekklēsia*: ministering saints and mature disciples. This follows from Jesus' departing mandate to the eleven (Matt. 28:16-

20): "Go and make disciples." The basic commission was not to preach sermons, not to plant churches, not to become notable clergypersons, not to evangelize (though that followed). No! Instead: "Go and make disciples." The Greek word here is *mathēteusate*. We are to *call* people to be attached to Jesus himself, to obey him in all of life, to do the deeds of Christ, and to be ready to suffer with him. To be a disciple, one must be called; we must give that call and develop mature followers of Jesus.

Disciple-making is an obvious concept in the New Testament, but I almost backed into it. We want all the baptized to live and think Christianly. But the traditions of churches depersonalize this concept. They substitute large public gatherings and lectures for personal involvement, responsibility, and accountability. This also separates clergy from laity, enabling clergy to live in their world and laity in another. It has produced a large professing Christian community which is saltless salt and hidden light (Matt. 5:13-16).

A new understanding dawned on me as I thought of those I had influenced as pastor and teacher. My pulpit teaching was not crucial (though that was a factor). I was more effective in the one-on-one or small-group time I spent with people in intense interaction over the Word of God: a high school student who hung around me a lot; a financial officer with whom I often drank coffee; a university student who attached himself to me; a group who helped me study and prepare my sermons; and a freewheeling house church called Kelly's Bible Study.

Henrietta Mears was a towering example of disciple-making in my tradition. She was director of Christian education in the large Hollywood First Presbyterian Church, teaching the college class, and spending early Saturday mornings with leaders of that group in an intense disciple-making role. The fruit of that ministry is everywhere today, in seminary and college teaching slots, in key pulpits and chaplaincies. Mears' spiritual children practiced what they learned and now have spiritual children and grandchildren of their own.

Another from my tradition is Robert Boyd Munger. As a pastor and seminary teacher, he discipled untold numbers of men and women. He touched their lives with the Word of God.

From a biblical perspective, the meaning of disciple-making is obvious: the Lord said, Go, and do with others what I have done with you. Gather a small number of willing persons to spend significant time with you (or maybe they will call you). *Let them get close and get to know the real you.* Let them ask questions and raise objections. Teach them the gospel of the kingdom. Show them how it is lived. Be a model for them. Then coach them and send them out to disicple others. Call them back and refine them. Reflection, action, reflection, as in the Christian base communities of Latin America.

Each disciple can in turn disciple others, until the whole world is discipled. In Ephesians 4, the pastor-teacher is a disciple-maker. Paul gives Timothy the same message: "What you have heard from me through many witnesses entrust to faithful people who will be able to teach others as well" (2 Tim. 2:2, NRSV).

Paul may sound arrogant: "Whatever you have learned or received or heard from me, or seen in me—put it into practice. And the God of peace will be with you" (Phil. 4:9). Yet that is not arrogance. It is teaching and modeling the new life in Christ, making "the life of Jesus . . . visible" (2 Cor. 4:10, NRSV). It is legitimate and faithful disciple-making, obedience to Christ. As Paul says, "Follow my example, as I follow the example of Christ."[2]

The people of God, the laity, need pastoral leaders to help them interact with Scriptures and process their real lives. They need a place of closeness and of intimacy. They need a disciple-maker. Missiological eyes see how critical this is. Scripture is not preoccupied with large lecture halls, though they may be significant (Acts 19:9). If folk are to come to maturity in Christ, they need to talk about the horror stories, the sticky problems of daily life, the doubts and questions that plague them. They need to do it in a friendly context with Scripture as a word from the Lord.

Otherwise, a church goes on, vulnerable to every doctrinal wind that blows. The mission will never be carried out if no one is brought to maturity to obey the mandate. This is why North American workplaces, though inhabited by many church members, are influenced so little by their presence.

Christians overcome by the word of their testimonies. If the kingdom pastors are to be servants of the Word and base-builders, they will have to mix it up with people. The pastor has to love the Word and the people, and bring those two loves together. No more of this aloof clergy stuff! I used to have a daily coffee klatch at a nearby university. Often divinity school folk joined us. I cringed as they frequently stressed that clergy must maintain their "ministerial mystique" and not become too familiar with congregational members. What an aberration from Jesus, who spent at least two years living with his disciples! Pastoral ministry requires not mystique but intimacy and vulnerability and modeling.

Too few seminaries have courses in disciple-making. Ministry after the example of Jesus calls us out of the hallowed precincts of our study and gets us intensely involved with people. We do this not as experts and teachers but as models, as real people, as base-builders, practitioners of the Word we teach.[3] For heaven's sake, people in the church need models! They need to see the kingdom lifestyle fleshed out. Folk don't identify with the great saints in the past or far away. They identify with people they see and know. Otherwise the whole Christian kingdom enterprise is unreal.

Although pastors and elders can be primary models, God raises up other models in unexpected ways and places. People in the church, especially youth, look around. If all they see is a group of immature, bored, church members, they think, "Who needs this?" But if there is a disciple-maker or group of disciple-makers possessed by the Word and joy of the gospel, they take a step closer to find out what is going on.

Lesslie Newbigin describes the congregation as "the hermeneutic of the gospel" to the world—that which interprets the gospel to the unbelieving community. A disciple-maker is also a hermeneutic of the gospel. In her life, the joyous news of the dominion of God in Jesus Christ is made real and interpreted in flesh-and-blood terms.

We're looking for people who are mature in Christ, who know who Jesus is, and who become his contemporary incarnation. They walk out into the Monday morning world, amidst the catch-22 enigmas of secular society and the ethical questions of corporate North America, as salty-salt and burning lights, nothing less.

Disciple-making Groups

Corporate worship does have exciting potential in creating a community rich in the Word of Christ. But in smaller, more informal, and intimate groups, Scriptures take on flesh and blood, the realities of the incarnation. In disciple-making real struggling human beings interact with the dynamic of Scriptures to have lives formed and transformed by those Scriptures. Disciple-making creates other disciple-makers.

I look for or create such groups. My church leadership is one such group. Our elders and deacons aren't only organizational necessities but brothers and sisters growing into discipleship with me. If we are immature in Christ, then the whole congregation will probably be immature. We spend time together apart from necessary business, growing in the Word.

When I arrive in a church community, I often invite people in the church to contract to spend a number of Sunday evenings with me at my home studying and discussing Scripture. There are always some unexpected jewels, who respond. It is significant time spent in Scriptures, in the warmth of a home. We create friends, disciples, growth, mutual understanding, and disciple-makers.

I always teach the membership class for new and prospective members. This gives me relaxed, informal, relational time with those coming into the church.

Prayer groups, luncheon groups, elective classes, intentional discipleship groups—all are occasions for the close-up, teach-model-coach ministry of base-building. The word of testimony becomes the word of Christ dwelling richly in a congregation. Light is generated, and Satan's darkness is dispelled. Kingdom community is created by the Word of God. The dragon is overcome!

Beware of any attractive subversion which distracts you from your calling to disciple-making, for it is by this ministry that we overcome. It looks so undramatic, but it is what Jesus mandates us to do. This is why Satan resists it so perennially and subtly. There are Achor churches because pastors came and left—and no one made disciples. When you leave a church, have you left disciples formed by the Word, able to make (and are making) disciples?

Worship, Preaching, Lord's Supper, Baptism

Public worship is not the primary place for disciple-making. It is too large and impersonal. But worship is a visible setting in our ecclesiastical pattern, the one time and place when the whole church family gathers. Thus it has great potential for base-building, whether in congregations of fifty or five thousand. That sounds self-evident. But worship can be tragically detached from any incarnational reality unless we see it also through the lenses of the Vision and of the laity.

Our goals in worship must be that we have a living, breathing encounter with God; that the word of our testimony and the Word of Christ be rich and compelling; that nothing be perfunctory or sterile; and that everything relate to daily life and equip for real life in the Monday-morning world. Kingdom pastors must therefore be worshipers in truth before they become worship leaders. They must stand awed and be evangelized by what they enact in worship. "Come, Creator Spirit!"

Every part of the worship service can be nurturing, since in theory it all flows from the Scriptures, whether the call to worship, a prayer of adoration, readings, confession, absolution, hymns, ceremonies, sermon, and responses. The Lord gathers his people from a week of being scattered in a confusing world. God wants to meet with us by his Word and Spirit. God wants us to know him as he is, to see his glory, and to regain our true perspective for our earthly sojourn. God forgives, encourages, and equips us. Then God scatters us again into the world as his ministers of the new covenant. The worship service should be large-scale base-building and disciple-making time. Here again is the pattern of reflection, action, reflection.

Preaching often becomes a pastor's idol more than deliberate disciple-making and base-building. One cynical laymen told me that he felt that every preacher he knew was preaching, not to equip the congregation, but to please seminary professors he hadn't seen in years. Lord, have mercy! Face it! You have maybe twenty minutes for teaching the Word to a congregation that just read the Sunday funnies and the sports page. The challenge must be faced realistically. The content of your sermon is important, but your own realism and captivation by the Word also communicates. Your mission is to infect people with your contagious thrill with the Word of Christ and to create in them a hungering and thirsting for the Word which will drive them to study it. Then the sermon is worth it.

However, God's people must be able to look beyond the pew, the pulpit, and the sermon. They must see how the sermon equips them in Christ for the realities of Monday, if the Word, the Lord's Supper, and baptism are to be effective means of grace.

When a congregation is biblically astute, the lectionary gives a good framework for preaching. But the lectionary assumes considerable familiarity with biblical context. Some clergy love the lectionary because it saves them the discipline of planning. However, laity are often confused by the somewhat random texts, many of which are unfamiliar.

I find consecutive exposition of books or larger segments of the Bible more useful and satisfying in base-building from the pulpit. I learned this from the evangelical Anglicans.[4] Preaching week after week from a given book of the Bible creates a climate of understanding and an increasing experience of that Scripture. My congregations kid me about my endless exposition of Matthew and the Sermon on the Mount. Yet one listener added, "But I must say that I am beginning to think and feel and respond in life to the Sermon on the Mount." Yes! That's the point!

When sermons are confusing to the laity, preaching obscures rather than enlightens. When the Word of God is trivialized, darkness intrudes. When sermons are subjective whims of the preacher and do not deal seriously with the Word of Christ, no base is built. You get Christian Faith Lite! Kingdom pastors can do better than that.

They Do Not Love Their Lives First

There are two ways to come at this final weapon of our warfare. One way is to say again that where the *message* of the blood and the Word are faithfully heralded, taught, used, and made focal, the *messenger,* the kingdom pastor (or any Christian using weapons of spiritual warfare) may become the target of irrational attacks. She may be the target of lies, accusations, emotional darkness, family disasters, and other suffering. He may face whatever weapons will disable, discredit, or discourage him. Church history is strewn with heartbreaking stories of gifted and faithful messengers who were casualties, unexpectedly and irrationally.[5]

Another way to come at this is by the more personal and subjective door of *sanctification.* Overcomers do "not love their lives so much as to shrink from death" (Rev. 12:11). They are baptized into Christ and consciously into Christ's death, and so count themselves dead to sin, to the world. They are already crucified with Christ! (cf. Rom. 6:1-14; Gal. 2:20; Col. 2:12). Jesus' invitation in the gospels always includes the call to discipleship: "If any want to become my followers, let them deny themselves and take up their cross daily and follow me. For those who want to save their life will lose it, and those who lose their life for my sake will save it" (Luke 9:23-24, NRSV).

We are talking about the *cruciform* life, life shaped by the cross of Jesus. The world considers such a life a foolish waste. The world may reject one who sacrifices career for obedience to the gospel. Such a life requires real conversion. It becomes personal. The call is to a radical conversion to Christ and death to self for Jesus' sake! This is truly what it means to be a Christian.

The blood and the Word have power to overcome. In the gospel enterprise, this power is expressed in the overcoming lives that are so identified with Christ that they are marked by the cross. Radical conversion to Jesus! The seductions faced by the pastor in the Valley of Achor are subtle: avoidance of suffering, "I deserve better" self-pity, puffed-up self-esteem, upward mobility, priority on providing for family. All these traps consign the church to Satan and display the pastor's self-love. Evil then prevails.

The conversion must be a joyous one, shared by kingdom pastor, spouse, and family. Maybe this is why Paul apparently stayed single! The calling and the conversion must be shared, but not with grim and joyless resignation. This is a calling to death to self. "Unless a kernel of wheat falls to the ground and dies, it remains only a single seed. But if it dies, it produces many seeds" (John 12:24). The implications of that are clear to the person who offers a burning heart to God.

However, we have developed a clergy culture that stands in stark contrast to Christ. In the wilderness, Jesus resisted the lures of this age: wealth (bread), influence (the kingdoms of this world), and fame (temple spectaculars). He chose poverty, weakness, hiddeness—and a cross. That sort of thing is not in high demand in clergy ranks. We are speaking of a death to clergy idols, to power and influence, to salary and upward mobility, to being called reverend and doctor, to self-pity, to reputation, to faithlessness, to clergy elitism, and to success.

Kingdom pastors and overcomers recognize the clash of kingdoms. They are converted to the radical gospel of the kingdom of God. They know spiritual conflict comes with the territory. Like Paul, they are converted, not to a clergy career, but to Christ. Thus, in whatsoever state they find themselves, they may be content (Phil. 4:11).

They are converted to Christ so that they share in his sufferings in the Valley of Achor.[6] They can abound and be abased without losing their spiritual balance. They can be "nobodies" or "somebodies" with equal joy, thanksgiving, and humility. Theirs is a conversion to a life and an adventure "too wild and free for the timid."[7] It is a conversion to holiness, to worship in the Spirit, and to being midwives of renewal for Valley of Achor congregations. Above all, it is a conversion to follow the "slaughtered" Lamb of God (Rev. 5:12, NRSV).

Only by such death and resurrection are we free to be kingdom pastors. Only then can we be free to love, free to listen, free to be *for* the people in the Valley of Achor, free to "spend and be spent" (2 Cor. 12:15), free to discern the spirits and the subversion, free to sing, dance, and celebrate—free to live Christ. Yes, free to be troubadours of God, cocreators with God, parenting kingdom colonies (1 Cor. 4:15), doors of hope, in the most unlikely places.

This death-conversion is celebrated continually in the observance of baptism. I become excited at every baptism because conversion, death, and resurrection are so graphic there. The Romans 6 imagery throbs with power, confronting us with our dying with Christ and being "buried with him through baptism into [his] death in order that, just as Christ was raised from the death through the glory of the Father, we too may live a new life." In my tradition, the questions that go along with baptism begin with a renunciation of Satan:

Do you desire to be baptized?
Do you renounce Satan and all the spiritual forces of wickedness that rebel against God?
Do you renounce the evil powers of this world which corrupt and destroy the creatures of God?
Do you renounce all sinful desires that draw you from the love of God?

Kingdom pastors also renounce Satan and his nonredemptive accusations about us, about the church, and about the people of the church. When we renounce his subversion, we can joyously affirm the rest of the baptismal questions.

Do you turn to Jesus Christ and accept him as your Savior?
Do you put your whole trust in his grace and love?
Do you promise to follow and obey him as your Lord?

Only thus are kingdom pastors free to be overcomers, to sculpt the Vision because they do not love their own lives so much that shrink from death. With integrity they are agents of God's new creation in Christ.

"I'm *spent,*" Debbie confessed, "so I guess I am like the apostle Paul, after all. It's overwhelming. No wonder we lost the Vision and felt frustrated, seduced, and bewildered so quickly. I was never given such a perspective of pastoral ministry in the design of God. I only hope I'm ready for the consequences. I desperately need you guys to pray for me. I will certainly pray for you."

"I didn't know what I was getting into when I dredged up old Franz Overbeck, did I?" said Andy. "Sounds like he had encountered Christian Faith Lite. I wonder if he knew what he was saying. This is not easy, but it sure makes sense biblically."

"I may be the most vulnerable of us," Ben worried. "Mammon is a cruel taskmaster. But I really do believe that

God loves these rich but often-brokenhearted and frequently empty folk with whom I live and minister. The challenge of being a kingdom pastor there is interesting to contemplate. But I need to dwell in the secret place of the Most High more intentionally, don't I?"

"Yes, we all do," I encouraged them.

I went back to Revelation 1. Even in the most tragic scenes of Revelation, there float the strains of "Worthy is the Lamb, who was slain, to receive power and wealth and wisdom and strength and honor and glory and praise!" (5:12).

Note that the apostle John has grace to see all of this overview of the church in history because he is in the Spirit on the Lord's Day (Rev. 1:10). He is worshiping in the Spirit. In that state of being at one with the Spirit of glory and of God, he is shown what it means. He is in exile, in a prison camp, but he sees the pretenses of the Beast and the true end of all things and the power of the Lamb. That eschatalogical Vision and perspective gets lost unless we worship, keep in view the cross and the Word, and love not our lives first. We don't want the Vision to get lost in the battle with the beast.

Conclusion

The human impossibility of the kingdom pastor's calling makes it so thrilling. Yes! Paul assures us that the "weapons we fight with are not the weapons of the world. On the contrary, they have divine power to demolish strongholds" (2 Cor. 10:4).

We have described those weapons of divine power. They go together. When the weapons are used patiently, boldly, and prayerfully, Achor is replaced by Hope, and heaven sings for joy! We have talked about the spiritual weapons of the blood of the Lamb, the Word of testimony, and loving not our lives even unto death. We have also looked at ministry through the eyes of the laity and the eyes of the mission which God assigned to the church. Whether overtly or subtly, angrily or seductively, the forces of evil will attack us at the precise points where we use these weapons.

We will never do this perfectly. We will often doubt if we are doing it at all. We will frequently not recognize the miracle of the new creation when it happens. This is what *grace* is all about. God reads your heart, and God loves you. Often you will discern God's wonderful workings much better in retrospect.

Our pilgrimage in this book has taken us from Annie Dillard's frog sucked empty by the giant waterbug, to three pastors in tears, to a journey through the wilderness of our conflict (cf. Mark 1:12-13). On the way, we have seen God's Vision, the pattern given on the mount, and heard the shout of heaven from those who are overcomers. Andy's discovery of Overbeck is timely. The church is called by our Lord Jesus to be the *community of the age to come*. Yet it so quickly accommodates itself again to *this present evil age*. Hope becomes Achor all too swiftly.

The kingdom pastor has a zeal for the honor of God's name—a high and holy calling. I have addressed this book primarily to the church in North America, which may be one of the most subverted continents. Lesslie Newbigin said[8] that the two cultures in the world most resistant to the gospel of the kingdom are Europe and the United States. Other observers corroborate this decline of the church in the West. As I write this, the church is emerging with new luster and power in tragic, oppressive, often-tumultuous nations. I see the faithful witness where life is so tragic, and my heart thrills, my eyes fill with tears.

However, I am not there, in Smyrna or Philadelphia, in their poverty, suffering, and faithfulness (Rev. 2–3). I am in North America, in Laodicea, with wealth and indifference to Christ outside the door. As the darkness intensifies, it becomes clearer that the Christian community is needed, to encourage the saints crying, "How long?" (Rev. 6:10). The shape and form of these wineskin-communities may and will change, but the calling to God's kingdom pastors does not.

Darkness will always seek to quench the Spirit and obscure the Vision. There will always be subtle or blatant attacks on the blood of the Lamb and the Word of God. There will be seductive pressure for us to accept mere custodial roles in religious communities congenial to Christian Faith Lite. This, however, is where God has called us to kingdom faithfulness—and to himself.

> And though this world with devils filled,
> Should threaten to undo us,
> We will not fear, for God hath willed
> His truth to triumph through us.
> The prince of darkness grim—
> We tremble not for him;
> His rage we can endure,
> For lo, his doom is sure;
> One little word shall fell him.
>
> That word above all earthly powers,
> No thanks to them, abideth;
> The Spirit and the gifts are ours
> Thru Him who with us sideth.
> Let goods and kindred go,
> This mortal life also:
> The body they may kill:
> God's truth abideth still,
> His kingdom is forever. Amen.
>
> (Martin Luther on Psalm 46)

Even so, Lord Jesus, come in! Stand outside no longer. Come and sit at table with us. Give us ears to hear, and make us your overcomers. This sojourn with the risen Lord is the Patmos where you and I walk with him and he with us. It is here that God wills his glory—not just at some later date. Our walk with the risen Christ is real here and now. He is faithful and true. To him be all praise! Amen.

• • •

This composite but not fictitious dialogue with Ben, Debbie, and Andy ended with worship. So may the sojourn of all the real Bens, Debbies, and Andys begin with worship which sees the Vision of God's purpose in glory for communities of the dominion of God. May it end in worship which gives adoration to the God who calls us to an experience of his faithfulness. Let that be so even if we literally or figuratively lose our lives in the process.

10

Epilogue: The Order of Shammah

TO BEN, Debbie, Andy, and their pastoral counterparts, I send this word of hope and this call to kingdom integrity, to kingdom pastorates. Yet all this armor and battlefield talk doesn't seem to fit us. We sing, "Encamped along the hills of light, ye Christian soldiers rise, and press the battle ere the night shall veil the glowing skies." Our hearts feel warm and we feel good; then comes the drudgery of Tuesday mornings, and we wonder, "What was all that about?"

It doesn't help to see Romero or Tutu or Popieluzko as examples, because that's not who we are and that's not where we live. The principle we accept is this: wherever I am, there is both my sanctuary and my battlefield. There I am the embodiment of Christ, to be God's glory. If not, I am still part of the darkness!

Mennonite, Roman Catholic, Presbyterian, Bible Church, or Pentecostal—it's all the same church and the same battle. The calling doesn't mean we forsake excellence or become resident critics of Achor. Wherever we are, in a sleepy town, in a decaying city, or in a tall-steeple Laodicea, our Lord calls us to be a troubadour of God.

A kingdom pastor is a *Shammah!* Shammah is the patron saint of lonely warriors, David's mighty man of valor —Shammah, son of Agee the Hararite. Shammah faced a field full of Philistines. He was forsaken by the other troops of Israel, yet assigned to that place by David. He was scared, faithful, obedient, bold (maybe even angry at the others and at David). He defended that plot of lentils, struck down the Philistines, and the Lord wrought a great victory (2 Sam. 23:11-12).

On tens of thousands of lonely spiritual battlefields (called churches) stand Shammah's lonely counterparts. Some places look prosperous and are poor. Some look nightmarish and are. Nevertheless, our great king sends his Shammahs there to create pockets of life, to nourish pools of living water, to establish colonies of the kingdom of God. "The Lord is There (*Yahweh-Shammah*)" (Ezek. 48:35), and the church, the new Jerusalem, is coming (Gal. 4:26; Rev. 21:2, 10).

Let us create the Noble Order of Shammah for those who, by design or call or the gracious providence of the sovereign Lord, are in lonely plots of lentils and take their stand there. When seduction tempts or others flee, *there with Christ* they stand!

We have the promise of Jesus: "I am with you always, to the end of the age" (Matt. 28:20). In that lonely place, the Shammahs see not only the Valley of Achor but also and especially the Door of Hope. Because the Creator God is bringing in his new creation. Hallelujah!

> Yours, O Lord, is the greatness and the power and the glory and the majesty and the splendor, for everything in heaven and earth is yours. Yours, O Lord, is the kingdom; you are exalted as head over all. (1 Chron. 29:11)

> Worthy is the Lamb, who was slain, to receive power and wealth and wisdom and strength and honor and glory and praise! (Rev. 5:12)

You, O Lord, are with me, in me, and for me. Here I stand, with you, the Overcomer!

May the God of peace fill you with praise, give you mirth and joy in your calling, crush Satan under your feet (Rom. 16:20), and give you many disciples as your reward. Yes, and a great victory, a Door of Hope. Amen.

Notes

Preface

1. Neuza Itioka, "Mission in the 1990s," *International Bulletin of Missionary Research* 14/1 (1990): 7-10.

Chapter 1: Kingdom and Conflict in Pastoral Ministry

1. Annie Dillard, *Pilgrim at Tinker Creek* (New York, N.Y.: Bantam Books, 1982).

2. *Heilgeschichte* means the story of God's saving work as recorded in Scripture.

3. Gabriel Fackre, *The Story of Salvation* (Grand Rapids: Eerdmans, 1984), uses the word *Vision* (capitalized) to express God's vision for the world, the kingdom of God, God's shalom. I have borrowed that usage here.

4. Karl Barth, *The Epistle to the Romans* (New York, N.Y.: Oxford University Press, 1980), in his preface to the second edition makes this passing reference to Franz Overbeck, which I have picked up and woven through this book. On "this present age" and "the age to come," see Mark 10:30; Eph. 1:21; 2:7; "this present evil world/age": 1 Cor. 1:20; 2:6; 2 Cor. 4:4; Gal. 1:4; Eph. 2:2; Titus 2:12; "the coming age": Heb. 6:5; overlapping, the new age/dominion/creation invading the old: Mark 1:15; John 1:5, 10-12; 12:31-32; 1 Cor. 10:11; 2 Cor. 5:17; Col. 1:13; etc.

5. If my readers need a gimmick to help describe the personality of these three caricatured congregations, try these first-century groups in Israel: *Sadducee party*, wealthy merchant and priestly class which tipped its hat to the Torah and the temple establishment, but used the temple for economic gain (Ben's congregation); *Pharisee party*, religious

nationalists, who saw purity of faith and national interest as dependent upon one another, like modern "Bible and flag" patriots (Andy's church); the *Essenes* and the Qumran community (known through the Dead Sea Scrolls), so absorbed with their own holiness and proper ritual in obedience to the Torah, and with purifying temple and priesthood (Debbie's congregation). Perhaps some present radical liberationist folk could be likened to *zealots*!

Traits of such parties frequently appear in contemporary congregations. In his mission to create a new humanity, Jesus said, "None of the above."

6. *Eschatalogical* derives from the Greek *eschatos*, "the last." It deals with what happens at the end-time or with the deepest purpose and destiny of a thing. I use it to draw attention to the ultimate purpose of the church in the mind of God and to the church as the community of the age to come.

Chapter 2: It's Not Neutral Out There

1. G. K. Chesterton, *St. Francis of Assisi* (New York, N.Y.: Image Books, 1957), 66.

2. Fackre, *The Story of Salvation*.

3. Missiologist Jonathan Bonk says, "Those who follow Christ are not only pilgrims and strangers on this earth, but we are soldiers behind the lines in enemy territory—at great peril, engaged in a life-and-death struggle to wrest territory away from an enemy who—in the words of our Scriptures—is ruler of this dark world. . . . The church is engaged in mortal combat against an enemy who will give no quarter; no prisoners are taken; there is no neutral zone; no treaty is possible." In *Toward the 21st Century in Christian Mission*, ed. J. Phillips and R. Coote (Grand Rapids: Eerdmans, 1993), 301.

4. Franz Overbeck, quoted in Barth, *The Epistle to the Romans*.

Chapter 3: Achor and Hope

1. These are deliberate caricatures and not exact copies of any particular church. In every congregation there is too much ambiguity to see it as consistent with any caricature. In the worst congregations there is evidence of grace; in the best there is always something despicable.

2. The Hosea reference to hope in the Valley of Achor is most colorful. In the Valley of Achor, or Trouble, the Israelites under Joshua stoned Achan and his family for bringing trouble upon Israel. This beautiful promise says that even in such a place, God will bring newness and hope.

3. A usage from Walter Brueggemann's writings.

4. God calls his people to become an alternative community which lives in the prospect of Christ's return and the consummation of God's purpose in Christ. The church is to be a people of hope, alien to

this present world scene. Otherwise, it becomes part of the darkness, or according to Overbeck, demonic.

5. J. B. Phillips, *New Testament Christianity* (New York, N.Y.: Macmillan, 1966), 2.

6. There are delicate and indelicate translations of the Greek word *skubalon* in Phil. 3:8. The sanitized RSV says "refuse," the NEB "garbage," the NIV and REB "rubbish." The word has more graphic Anglo-Saxon translations and can mean "dung," say W. F. Arndt and F. W. Gingrich in *A Greek-English Lexicon of the New Testament and Other Early Christian Literature* (Chicago: Univ. of Chicago Press, 1957), 765. It is deliberately used here to describe a real dimension of Satan's assaults on God's faithful.

7. "The ends of the ages" have come upon us, and we are in the middle of the struggle between the two (1 Cor. 10:11, NRSV). In the dynamics of passages such as Eph. 2:1-10, Rom. 6, and Gal. 5:13-26, we see sources for behavior in the congregations. One source produces unrighteous behavior, while the other produces new-creation behavior, which is godlike.

8. Cf. Jacques Ellul's use in *The Subversion of Christianity* (Grand Rapids: Eerdmans, 1986), 19. This is a primary source for understanding the infiltration of disobedient culture into the church and of the church's response.

Chapter 4: The Community of the Great King

1. *Malkuth shamayim* (the kingdom of the heavens) is the Aramaic designation which Matthew (4:17) translates as "the kingdom of heaven." It was the hope or consolation of Israel, the trust in the coming reign or dominion of Yahweh. This hope, this *malkuth shamayim*, taught in the synagogues, was a common expectation of Israel. We see it in the godly Simeon, who looked for "the consolation of Israel" (Luke 1:25). cf. Dan. 4:;26, KJV, "The heavens do rule."

2. Designation attributed to sociologist Peter Berger.

3. Designation attributed to Old Testament scholar Walter Brueggemann.

4. From Lesslie Newbigin, *The Gospel in a Pluralist Society* (Grand Rapids: Eerdmans, 1989), 222ff.

5. From Stanley Hauerwas and William Willimon, *Resident Aliens* (Nashville, Tenn.: Abingdon, 1989).

6. Attributed to Søren Kierkegaard.

Chapter 5: The Pattern Given on the Mount

1. In the decades since this episode, the study of church administration has progressed by light years, with such superb resources as the Alban Institute and other agencies. These are to be commended.

2. The books have disappeared from my library, but I recall that

one was by Bakht Singh, an Indian leader, and the other was by Watchman Nee, a Chinese Christian.

3. I am often challenged by my usage of the verb *evangelize* with reference to people or congregations that already profess the gospel, the evangel. But *evangelize* is also a verb that speaks of the formation of a person or persons by that gospel, as Paul wishes to proclaim the gospel to the saints in Rome (cf. Rom. 1:7, 15). The faithful pastor is always evangelizing the congregation by continually attempting to form them into a living demonstration of the gospel of the kingdom of God.

4. I am assuming that the pastor-teacher is a single gift, though some commentators do not agree.

5. Congregations usually begin with a fairly clear sense of purpose and mission and are excited about it. The second generation carries on with a bit less motivation. By the third and fourth generation, church is often a tradition and a rite devoid of mission fervor. It is in a custodial or maintenance mode.

6. Ellul, *The Subversion of Christianity*, 190.

7. *Eisegesis* describes reading into the biblical text one's own meaning and making the text say what one has already decided, what is not really in the text.

8. Much of the present form of the church, and its self-understanding, comes from tradition out of post-Constantinian Christianity more than from Scripture. The life and form of the apostolic church appear quite fluid at times, except that they had a dynamic awareness and experience of the Holy Spirit and the Spirit's gifts. My own tradition of government by presbyters (Presbyterian) takes a leadership mentioned in the New Testament and universalizes it into a rigid form not always apparent in apostolic writings.

9. *Exegesis* describes attempts to find the meaning from the biblical text itself. It is the valid and necessary enterprise of students of the Bible. Exegetes subject themselves to the text of Scripture. Biblical exegesis may not be an adequate discipline by itself; there is a closely related discipline of *hermeneutics*, which has to do with the interpretation of the text. What were the circumstances and life setting in which this text was written? What are the circumstances and life setting in which we now hear it?

Exegesis is not simple. Some no longer trust the distinction between eisegesis and exegesis. In this book, I call the pastor to look at the Scripture and the pastoral ministry through *laity eyes* and through *missiological eyes;* we come to the text with a bias, looking for these interpretive points. Someone could call that eisegesis. However, a saving feature is for the interpreter to acknowledge one's own presuppositions and be open about testing to see whether they fit the Scripture and its message.

10. F. R. Maltby quoted in W. Barclay, *The Letters to the Galatians*

and Ephesians (Philadelphia, Pa.: Westminster Press, 1958), 146.

11. This renunciation is from *The Book of Common Prayer (Proposed)* of the Episcopal Church, 1977, but similar renderings exist in most liturgies of Protestant and Catholic churches. They are rooted in the baptismal formulas of the church in its first centuries.

12. Newbigin, *The Gospel in a Pluralist Society*, chapter 18. He lists six characteristics: (1) a community of praise, (2) a community of truth, (3) a community that does not live for itself but is deeply involved in the concerns of its neighborhood, (4) a community where men and women are prepared for and sustained in the exercise of priesthood in the world, (5) a community of mutual responsibility, and (6) a community of hope.

13. Cf. "*Doxa* (glory)" in *Theological Dictionary of the New Testament*, ed. G. Kittel, vol. 2 (Grand Rapids: Eerdmans, 1964), 250-251.

14. Faith, hope, and love are best recalled from 1 Corinthians 13:13, but they are also an axiom and a refrain that turns up often. We see it not only in Pauline writings but also in Petrine letters (Eph. 1:15-18; Col. 1:3-5; 1 Thess. 1:2-3; 2 Thess. 1:3-4; faith and love in 1 Tim. 1:15; 1 Pet. 1:20-22).

15. Poem and lyric by Arthur Campbell Ainger, 1894.

16. In *The Rule of St. Benedict*, there is clear accountability and responsibility to the community (cf. Matt. 18:15-20). The abbot and the council are selected to see that this is healthy and has integrity as a community of faith, worship, and obedience. In most congregations there is hardly any recognized authority and, hence, no accountability by anyone or to anyone or to the goals of the community of Christ. Autonomy reigns supreme for the most part, especially in North American consumer society. If any demands are made which disturb my autonomy, I switch to another church. This has tragic consequences. Cf. John H. Yoder, *Body Politics: Five Practices of the Christian Community Before the Watching World* (Nashville: Discipleship Resources, 1992), 1–13, "Binding and Loosing."

17. I cannot trace the source of this list of *marks*. I have heard of them and used them often. I asked others who have included them in their writings. We assume that they emerged in the milestone works on the nature and mission of the church sponsored by the World Council of Churches in the middle of the twentieth century. Perhaps they came from writings of C. H. Dodd and were developed by W. A. Visser 't Hooft and Lesslie Newbigin.

18. Stanley Hauerwas spells out this non-acceptance of the church in *Unleashing the Scripture* (Nashville: Abington, 1993), chapter 19. The goal is that "the world might know that God's kingdom is about a new age. It is a kingdom where people have been created to be gentle, as we are told in Philippians, even in a cruel world. That many will see such gentleness as judgment on cruelty is part of the witness. And they will want to kill us for our gentleness, but our gentleness is the way the

world knows that God has called us to peace in a world at war" (82).

19. Segundo Galilea, *The Beatitudes* (New York, N.Y.: Orbis, 1984).

Chapter 6: Pathologies in the Church

1. Overbeck, quoted in Barth, *Romans,* preface to second edition.

2. Søren Kierkegaard, *Attack Upon Christendom* (Boston, Mass.: Beacon, 1944).

3. Hauerwas and Willimon, *Resident Aliens*. Stanley Hauerwas, *After Christendom* (Nashville: Abingdon, 1991).

4. The NEB translates the Greek word *sarkos* as "merely human"; the RSV and others translate it as "flesh" or "carnal."

5. "Apostolate" is not common currency in Protestant circles, but it is in Roman Catholic circles. It means one's mission or particular place of ministry. I have not found a good counterpart in Protestant life.

6. Hans Küng, *The Church* (New York, N.Y.: Sheed and Ward, 1967), 191ff.

7. Those who propose such transformation and change are seldom pastors of churches. They are usually leaders of institutes, teachers in seminaries or graduate schools, or in a place where it is safer to make such disruptive suggestions.

8. Within the past decade, telling studies have been written. I recommend Orlando Costas, *Christ Outside the Gate* (Maryknoll, N.Y.: Orbis, 1982); Roof and McKinney, *American Mainline Religion* (New Brunswick, N.J.: Rutgers University Press, 1987); Alfred Krass, *Evangelizing Neo-Pagan North America* (Scottdale, Pa.: Herald Press, 1982); Lesslie Newbigin, *Foolishness to the Greeks* (Grand Rapids: Eerdmans, 1986).

9. Walter Wink's three volumes, *Naming the Powers, Unmasking the Powers,* and *Engaging the Powers* (Philadelphia, Pa.: Fortress, 1984, 1986, 1992) are recent provocative studies of this often perplexing biblical theme. Ellul has a strong chapter on the powers in *The Subversion of Christianity*. Earlier classical works include English Puritans: William Gurnall, *The Christian in Complete Armour;* and John Bunyan, *The Holy War.* I also found help in a work by a Disciples missionary, F. J. Huegel, *That Old Serpent the Devil.*

10. See Luke 10:18; John 12:31; Rom. 16:20; Col. 2:15; Rev. 20:2, 10; etc.

11. William Stringfellow, *An Ethic for Christians and Other Aliens in a Strange Land* (Waco, Tex.: Word Books, 1976). This was one of his favorite prophetic themes.

12. Wink, *Unmasking the Powers,* 69ff.

Chapter 7: Journey into Hope

1. Peter Kuzmic, evangelical theologian from Yugoslavia, makes a statement about the church in Europe that applies unmistakably to the

church in North America. He contends that "one of the most urgent tasks for both Western and Eastern churches is to recover the practical missionary ecclesiology, the missionary character of the believing community." He attributes this statement to Lesslie Newbigin, then adds that "churches have to recognize that faith is not automatically inherited from generation to generation and that the main task of the church is not its institutional and mechanistically sacramental self-perpetuation." In *Toward the 21st Century in Christian Mission*, 159.

2. I am not denigrating these resources, most of which I use and applaud. But by themselves, without Vision, they also fall short.

3. Kuzmic says, "Neither should the ministry of the clergy be reduced to the servicing of baptisms, weddings, and funerals. The church needs to be internally renewed by the power of the Holy Spirit, in order to become recognizable" as kingdom communities. In *Toward the 21st Century*, 159.

4. Donald Jacobs, in *Toward the 21st Century*, 235-236.

5. Paul tells believers in Rome that he wishes to come and evangelize them also (Rom. 1:7, 15). It is not only legitimate but expressive to speak of evangelizing and reevangelizing the church. It is an ongoing ministry. The Greek word *euangelizomai* means a thrilling announcement. It is our task to thrill God's people again and again with the thrilling words of Jesus and the gospel. This is undoubtedly what the late John Paul I meant when he said that the primary and urgent task of the church today is to "evangelize those already baptized."

6. P. T. Forsyth, *The Soul of Prayer* (London: Independent Press, 1954), 7ff.

7. Hauerwas and Willimon observe that "there is a condition much worse than being a 'failure'—namely, to be a 'success.' " *Resident Aliens*, 141.

8. I have been particularly blessed by Ministry of Money, a spin-off of the Church of the Saviour in Washington, D.C., which conducts intensive seminars on this area of struggle and publishes a periodical (2 Professional Drive, Suite 220, Gaithersburg, MD 20879-3420).

9. Newbigin makes this point: "The missionary encounter with our culture for which I am pleading will require *energetic fostering of a declericalized, lay theology*" (italics added). *Foolishness to the Greeks*, 142.

10. Brennan Manning has a poignant and helpful comment about vulnerability: "God entered into our world, not with a crushing impact of unbearable glory, but in the way of weakness, vulnerability, and need. On a wintry night in an obscure cave, the infant Jesus was a humble, naked, helpless God who allowed us to get close to him. We all know how difficult it is to receive anything from someone who has all the answers, who is completely cool, utterly unafraid, needing nothing, and in control of every situation. . . . So God comes as a newborn baby, giving us a chance to love him, making us feel that we have something

to give him. The world does not understand vulnerability." *Lion and Lamb* (Old Tappan, N.J.: Chosen, 1986), 175.

11. Rev. 1:19—3:22; Wink, *Naming the Powers*, 22ff., esp. 95-96.

12. Forsyth, 87.

13. Eugene Peterson has opened this passage more helpfully than any I know in his *Reversed Thunder* (San Francisco: Harper & Row, 1988), especially in chapter 7, "The Last Word on Prayer."

14. Forsyth, 23.

Chapter 8: Overcoming

1. Neuza Itioka, "Mission in the 1990s," *International Bulletin of Missionary Research*, 14/1 (1990): 7-10.

2. Accepting our faith in the sovereignty of God and his good purpose in Christ, we have to accept also that Satan is subject to this good purpose in Christ. Wink traces the teaching of Christ from Old Testament sources, where Satan is one of the angels of God (Job 1), to the role of Satan in the New Testament. He observes that Satan is like God's overzealous quality-control agent. God can use his accusing attacks and destructive work as part of our sanctification.

3. Ellul, *The Subversion of Christianity*, 19.

4. David Bosch says, "Martin Kähler suggested that mission was 'the mother of theology' or of the New Testament: it was because of their involvement in mission that the early Christians began to theologize. . . . Moreover, writes Heinrich Kasting, 'Mission was, in the early stages, . . . a fundamental expression of the life of the church. The beginnings of a missionary theology are therefore also the beginnings of Christian theology as such.' " "Missions in the 21st Century," in Phillips and Coote, *Toward the 21st Century*, 177.

5. Ellul, *The Subversion of Christianity*, 190.

6. Church-growth persons often talk as though it were unacceptable for folk to leave the church out of discontent. While the kingdom pastor will be an instrument of grace, it is also true that the Word of God has a double-edged effect. There is sifting and separating as kingdom communities emerge. "They went out from us, but they did not really belong to us. For if they had belonged to us, they would have remained with us; but their going showed that none of them belonged to us" (1 John 2:19).

Chapter 9: Disciple-making, Preaching, Cross-bearing

1. Newbigin says, "Theology has been the preserve of those who minister as priests and pastors to the inner spiritual life of their people. Consequently, when theologians whose sole work is in this pastoral ministry try to speak about matter of politics and economics, their words do not carry weight. . . . Christian men and women who are deeply involved in secular affairs view theology as the arcane pursuit of

professional clergymen. . . . The missionary encounter with our culture for which I am pleading will require *the energetic fostering of a declericalized, lay theology*" (italics added). Newbigin, *Foolishness to the Greeks,* 142.

2. On Paul calling himself an example, see also Acts 20:35; 1 Cor. 4:16; Phil. 3:17; 1 Thess. 1:6; 2 Thess. 3:7, 9; 1 Tim. 1:16.

3. The really effective communicating professors are not just gifted academically; they have been discipled and are therefore available to invest themselves in their students. They are not shy about sharing their own humanity and sojourn with Jesus Christ. Hence, students are interacting not so much with a seminary professor as with a brother or sister in Christ, one who is gifted and has proved his or her gifts.

4. Consecutive exposition was Calvin's practice and a major instrument in the reform of whole cultures by his influence. I was introduced to the practice by Anglican friends John R. W. Stott and J. Alec Motyer. More recently I have been blessed in my own tradition by the model of Frederick Dale Bruner, who rings this theme persistently in his monumental two-volume commentary on Matthew, *The Christ Book: Matthew 1-12,* and *The Church Book: Chapters 13-28* (Grand Rapids: Eerdmans, 1987, 1990). Another model is Earl Palmer of University Presbyterian Church in Seattle. I am certain there are more such expositors.

5. This shows the relevance of my former comment about the desirability of the kingdom pastor having a back-up or tent-making occupation. Otherwise, pastors under pressure may be tempted to make peace with evil at the expense of faithfulness and obedience. I know such a suggestion will not be well received. But as the dominion of Satan controls more churches in the United States, there will be more temptations and seductions to avoid conflict or unemployment by accommodating the neopaganism of the culture.

6. Sharing Christ's sufferings is discussed often in apostolic writings, including Rom. 8:17; Phil. 1:29; Col. 1:24; 2 Tim. 2:9-13; 1 Pet. 4:13; Rev. 5:12; 7:14; etc.

7. Phrase attributed to Madeline L'Engle regarding those who are too timid to get involved with Jesus Christ (especially among her literary colleagues).

8. Newbigen, *Foolishness to the Greeks.* Such resistance is the theme of this book.